by **Nick Schou**

KILL THE
MESSENGER

How the CIA's Crack-Cocaine Controversy Destroyed Journalist Gary Webb

NATION BOOKS · www.nationbooks.org · New York

Published by Nation Books,
A Member of the Perseus Books Group
116 East 16th Street, 8th Floor
New York, NY 10003
www.nationbooks.org

Nation Books is a co-publishing venture of the Nation Institute
and the Perseus Books Group
Copyright © Nick Schou 2006
Introduction © Charles Bowden 2006
Portions of Chapter 10 previously appeared in the OC *Weekly*
and the LA *Weekly*

Books published by Nation Books are available at special discounts for
bulk purchases in the United States by corporations, institutions, and
other organizations. For more information, please contact the Special
Markets Department at the Perseus Books Group, 2300 Chestnut Street,
Suite 200, Philadelphia, PA 19103, or call (800) 810-4145, ext. 5000, or
e-mail special.markets@perseusbooks.com.

Book design by Pauline Neuwirth, Neuwirth & Associates, Inc.

A CIP catalog record for this book is available from the
Library of Congress.
LCCN: 2007275820
ISBN 978-1-56025-930-5 (previous paperback edition)
ISBN 978-1-56858-471-3 (current paperback edition)
ISBN 978-0-78673-526-6 (e-book)

10 9 8 7 6 5 4 3 2 1

To Claudia and Erik,
for their love, support, and inspiration

CONTENTS

*Photo section appears between
pages 126 and 127*

INTRODUCTION

I MET HIM in a bar in Sacramento in April, 1998. His series on the CIA was almost two years old, and officially repudiated by the *Los Angeles Times, New York Times* and *Washington Post*. He'd lost his job and no one in the news business would hire him. I remember he entered the hotel saloon with a kind of swagger. I remember that he ordered Maker's Mark. And I remember idly mentioning conspiracy theories and that he instantly flared up and said, "I don't believe in fucking conspiracy theories, I'm talking about a fucking conspiracy."

I'd arrived there because early that winter at a New York restaurant I'd told a magazine editor that the only story worth writing about was: What in the hell had happened to Gary Webb? At that moment, I'd also said I thought his

series was true and the editor snapped, "Of course, it is." So
I'd spent months interviewing former DEA agents who'd
brushed against the CIA, devoured mountains of documents and become convinced that Webb's discredited series
was true. And that the papers and reporters who had
destroyed him were wrong.

I'd spent years bumbling around the drug world and anyone who does that runs into whiffs of the CIA that can never
be completely documented and that never seem to really go
away. I know a narc in Dallas who had seized over twenty
million dollars cash at the Dallas/Fort Worth airport from a
courier flying out of Miami and was told by the Justice
Department to return the money and let the man continue
on his way. I have a friend who witnessed the first non-stop
flight of cocaine and marijuana from Colombia to northern
Mexico in 1986, a full-bodied plane without seats that
landed at a desert airstrip. The pilot was from a CIA pro-
prietary company in Florida. My friend got time in a federal
prison. The pilot continued flying. I've talked to a DEA
agent who saw a plane full of cocaine land at a U.S. Air Force
base in the '80s. I've talked to a DEA agent who knew of
numerous drug fields in Mexico that handled drug flights
from Central America during the contra war and that were
never bothered by DEA.

You either dismiss these stories out of hand as impossible or you look into them and slowly but surely become convinced. I became convinced and accept the implication
that the CIA has for decades knowingly dealt with drug dealers and justified these actions by citing national security. Just
as they have dealt with other criminal syndicates. Gary

Webb stumbled upon one such instance, pursued it with tenacity, willed his account into print, and consequentially, was run out of the news business.

That's the guy I talked with in the bar in Sacramento. And that is the person you will meet in this book. He was the best investigative reporter I've ever known. But that hardly matters if you mess with our government's secret world without its consent.

When I met Webb I was deep into a book on the drug world of the U.S./Mexico border, a book that consumed almost eight years of my life. I amassed a lot of stuff on the CIA and drugs during those years, material I basically left out of the book because I did not want to become another Gary Webb and have my work pitched into the trash for the high crime of calling into question our national security bureaucracy.

So that's the deal: we now live in a country where reporters dread becoming Gary Webb. God help us.

When I first learned of his suicide, I shut down my life for two days, sat in my yard and drank. I'm not sure if I drank for Gary Webb or for the rest of us.

But I know Gary Webb got it right and that was the worst possible thing he could have done.

—CHARLES BOWDEN
2006

DRAMATIS PERSONAE

THE CONSPIRATORS

Danilo Blandon: Nicaraguan exile and cocaine trafficker, supplier of South Central dealer "Freeway" Ricky Ross. Became government informant against Ross.

Ronald Lister: Former Laguna Beach police detective, international arms merchant, security consultant and drug dealer with Blandon. Claimed to work for CIA.

Norwin Meneses: Known as King of drugs in Nicaragua during 1970s, major drug smuggler and supplier of Blandon.

"Freeway" Ricky Ross: First South Central crack dealer to become millionaire in 1980s. Sentenced to life in prison in 1996, but scheduled to be released from Lompoc Federal Penitentiary for good behavior in 2008.

THE OPERATORS

Adolfo Calero: CIA asset and political director of Nicaraguan Contras. Photographed with Meneses in San Francisco. Denied knowledge of drug dealing.

Roberto D'Aubuisson: Head of paramilitary death squads in El Salvador, business contact of Lister.

Enrique Bermudez: Contra commander and CIA asset who met with Blandon and Meneses in Honduras about fundraising, allegedly told them "ends justify the means." Shot to death in 1991 by unknown assailants in Nicaragua.

Tim Lafrance: San Diego weapons dealer who has worked with CIA. Traveled to El Salvador with Lister.

Bill Nelson: Former security director at Fluor Corp. in Orange County, ex-deputy director of operations for CIA. Business contact of Lister in 1980s. Died of natural causes in 1995.

Eden Pastora: Former Sandinista turned contra commander. Associate of Blandon.

Scott Weekly: U.S. intelligence operative, ex-soldier of fortune. Traveled to El Salvador with Lister.

THE WHISTLEBLOWERS

Jack Blum: Lead prosecutor for Senator John Kerry's probe of contra cocaine activity in 1980s.

Martha Honey: Former *New York Times* stringer based in Costa Rica. Unsuccessfully sued Reagan administration officials for role in bombing injuries suffered by her husband.

Peter Kornbluh: Director of the National Security Archive at George Washington University, which has declassified countless government documents from Iran contra era.

Bob Parry: Former AP and *Newsweek* reporter who authored the first stories involving contras and cocaine.

Michael Ruppert: Former Los Angeles police detective. Claimed he uncovered CIA ties to city's drug epidemic;

confronted CIA director John Deutch at South Central, L.A. town hall meeting.

Maxine Waters: L.A. Congresswoman who held hearings into CIA complicity with drug traffickers after "Dark Alliance."

THE MERCURY NEWS

Pete Carey: Veteran reporter assigned to investigate "Dark Alliance" after other papers criticized the series. Found no evidence of CIA involvement in drug ring.

Jerry Ceppos: Executive Editor who defended Webb, then published letter to readers backing away from "Dark Alliance."

Dawn Garcia: State Editor who worked directly with Webb on "Dark Alliance."

David Yarnold: Managing Editor who supervised "Dark Alliance." Stopped reading drafts halfway through editing process.

THE CRITICS

David Corn: Washington, D.C., editor of *The Nation*. Both criticized and defended "Dark Alliance."

Tim Golden: Former Central America correspondent for *Miami Herald*, wrote articles for *New York Times*, critical of "Dark Alliance."

Jesse Katz: *Los Angeles Times* writer who called Ross "mastermind" of crack cocaine two years before "Dark Alliance."

Joe Madison: National radio host also known as the "Black Eagle." Dedicated six months of daily coverage to "Dark Alliance," arrested outside CIA headquarters.

Doyle McManus: Washington Bureau Chief of the *Los Angeles Times*. Directed paper's response to "Dark Alliance."

Walter Pincus: Wrote articles critical of "Dark Alliance" for the *Washington Post*. Spied on student groups for CIA in 1950s.

Moving Day **ONE**

AFTER DAYS OF unrelenting winter rain from a powerful Pacific Storm, the clouds moved east and the skies cleared above the Sacramento valley. The snowcapped peaks of the western range of the Sierra Nevada glowed pink in the glinting early morning sun. On days like this, Gary Webb normally would have taken the day off to ride his motorcycle into the mountains.

Although it was a Friday morning, Webb didn't need to call in sick. In fact, he hadn't been to work in weeks. When his ex-wife garnished his wages seeking child support for their three kids, Webb asked for an indefinite leave from the small weekly alternative paper in Sacramento where he had been working the past four months. He told his boss he could no longer afford the $2,000 mortgage on his house in Carmichael, a suburb twenty miles east of the state capital.

There was no time for riding. Today, December 10, 2004, Webb was going to move in with his mother. It wasn't his first choice. First, he asked his ex-girlfriend if he could share her apartment. The two had dated for several months, and continued to live together until their lease expired a year earlier, when Webb had bought his new house. They had remained friends, and at first she had said yes, but she changed her mind at the last minute, not wanting to lead him on in the hope that they'd rekindle a romance.

Desperate, Webb asked his ex-wife, Sue, if he could live with her until he regained his financial footing. She refused. "I don't feel comfortable with that," she said.

"You don't?"

Sue recalls that her ex-husband's words seemed painfully drawn out. "I don't know if I can do that," she said. "Your mother will let you move in. You don't have any other choice."

Besides losing his house, Webb had also lost his motor-cycle. The day before he was to move, it had broken down as he was riding to his mother's house in a nearby retirement community. After spotting Webb pushing the bike off the road, a helpful young man with a goatee and a spider-web tattoo on his elbow had given him a lift home. Webb arranged to get a pickup truck, but when he went back to retrieve his bike, it had disappeared.

That night, Webb spent hours at his mother's house. At her urging he typed up a description of the suspected thief. But Webb didn't see much point in filing a police report. He doubted he'd ever see his bike again. He had been depressed for months, but the loss of his bike seemed to push him over the edge. He told his mother he had no idea how he was going to ever make enough money to pay child support and pay rent or buy a new home.

Although he had a paying job in journalism, Webb knew that only a reporting gig with a major newspaper would give him the paycheck he needed to stay out of debt. But after sending out fifty resumes to daily newspapers around the country, nobody had called for an interview. His current job couldn't pay the bills, and the thought of moving in with his mother at age forty-nine, was more than his pride would allow. "What am I going to do with the rest of my life?" he asked. "All I want to do is write."

It was 8 p.m. by the time Webb left his mother's house. She offered to cook him a dinner of bacon and eggs, but Webb declined, saying he had to go home. There were other things he had to do. She kissed him goodbye and told him to come back the next day with a smile on his face. "Things will be better," she said. "You don't have to pay anything to stay here. You'll get back on your feet."

The next morning, Anita Webb called her son to remind him to file a police report for the stolen bike. His phone rang and rang. She didn't bother leaving a message, figuring the movers already had arrived. They had. It's possible they heard the phone ring inside his house. As they approached his house, they noticed a note stuck to his front door. "Please do not enter," it warned. "Call 911 for an ambulance. Thank you."

When her son failed answer the phone for more than an hour, Anita Webb began to panic. Finally, she let the answering machine pick up. "Gary, make sure you file a police report," she said. Before she could finish, the machine beeped and an unfamiliar voice began to speak: "Are you calling about the man who lives here?"

It is normally the policy of the Sacramento County Coroner's office not to answer the telephone at the scene of a death, but apparently the phrase "police report" startled the coroner into breaking that rule. At some point early that morning, Gary Webb had committed suicide.

The coroners found his body in a pool of blood on his bed, his hands still gripping his father's 38-caliber pistol. On his nightstand were his social security card—apparently intended to make it easier for his body to be identified—a cremation card and a suicide note, the contents of which have never been revealed by his family. The house was filled with packed boxes. Only his turntable, DVD player, and TV were unpacked.

In the hours before he shot himself in the head, Webb had listened to his favorite album, *Ian Hunter Live*, and had watched his favorite movie, the Sergio Leone spaghetti western, *The Good, the Bad and the Ugly*. In a trashcan was a poster Webb had saved from his first journalism job with the *Kentucky Post*. The poster was an open letter to readers from Vance Trimble, Webb's first editor. Decades earlier, Webb had clipped it from the pages of the paper. Although he had always admired its message, something about it must have been too much to bear in his final moments. Trimble had written that, unlike some newspapers, the *Kentucky Post* would never kill a story under pressure from powerful interests. "There should be no fetters or reporters, nor must they tamper with the truth, but give light so the people will find their own way," his letter stated.

That morning, Sue Webb was at home in Folsom, just minutes away from Carmichael, when her cell phone started ringing. She was about to walk out the door to bring her fourteen-year-old daughter Christine to school. Because Sue was running late for a business meeting in Stockton, she didn't answer. But when she recognized the number of the caller as Kurt, her ex-husband's brother, she began to worry. "I was standing in the bathroom, and when I saw that number, I knew something had happened," she says. "I kept saying, 'No, this is not happening, this is not happening.' I was afraid to pick up the phone."

Thoughts raced through her mind. Two days earlier, Webb had taken Christine to a doctor's appointment. At the doctor's office, there was a copy of Dr. Seuss' *Green Eggs and Ham*, which Webb had loved reading to her years earlier. He jokingly asked her if she wanted him to read it aloud to her. When he dropped Christine off at Sue's house later that day, Christine said her father made a special point of walking up to the door to kiss her goodbye. "He told her to be good to her mom," Sue says. "And he handed her some little bottles of perfume and said 'I love you.' When she asked him if he wanted to come in, he said no."

Sue put her daughter in the car and drove a few blocks to the entrance of the middle-class neighborhood of tract houses where she lives on a wooded hillside on the outskirts of town. "I couldn't stand it anymore, because the phone kept ringing," she says. "It was Anita, and she was just sobbing. And I said, 'Is he gone?' and she said 'Yes.' And I just pulled off the road and started crying and said 'Christine, your daddy's dead.' We had to get out of the car and we sat on the grass together and just started crying. I don't even know how long we sat there."

A woman driving by pulled over and asked what was wrong. Sue gave her the number of the healthcare company where she worked as a sales agent. She asked the woman to call and let them know she wouldn't be able to keep her appointments that day. Then she called her twenty-year-old son Ian and Eric, her sixteen-year-old, who was already at school, to tell them to meet her and Christine at Anita's house. "I had to tell them on the phone what had happened because they wouldn't let me hang up," she says.

When she arrived at Anita's house, Ian was sitting on the front lawn, tears streaming down his face. "The police had already left," she says. "I told him not to go inside." A block away from the house was a bench with a view of a duck pond. The tranquil scene seemed surreal, dreamlike, frozen in time. "I remember feeling this sense of loss. It was the weirdest thing in the world. I had moved to California to be with Gary and had left my family behind and suddenly I felt alone. And I knew almost immediately that he had killed himself."

That afternoon, Sue met Kurt at the coroner's office. "They took us into a room and the coroner came in and told us that Gary had shot himself and what gun he had used," she says. "It was his dad's gun that he had found when he was a security guard at a hospital in Cincinnati. Some patient had left it there and his dad had kept it. He used to keep it under the bed. I'd get mad because we had kids and he'd stick it in the closet."

Kurt asked the coroner if he was certain it was a suicide. "There's no doubt in my mind," he answered. He added that sometimes, people who shoot themselves have bruises on their fingers from squeezing the trigger. Apparently the will to live is so strong that suicide victims often grip the gun so tightly and for so long they lose blood circulation in their hands. "Gary had bruises on his fingers," Sue says.

A few days later, four letters arrived at Sue's house, one each for her and the three kids. Webb had mailed them before he died. He sent a separate letter to his mother, and a last will and testament to his brother Kurt. He told his children that he loved them, that Ian would make a woman happy someday, and that he didn't want his death to dissuade Eric from considering a career in journalism. His will divided his assets, including his just-sold house, between his wife and children. His only additional wish was that his ashes be spread in the ocean so he could "bodysurf for eternity."

WHILE IT WAS Gary Webb who pulled the trigger, the bullet that ended his life was a mere afterthought to the tragic unraveling of one of the most controversial and misunderstood journalists in recent American history. A college dropout with twenty years of reporting experience and a Pulitzer Prize on his resume, Webb broke the biggest story of his career in August 1996, when he published "Dark Alliance," a three-part series for the *San Jose Mercury News* that linked the U.S. Central Intelligence Agency (CIA) to America's crack-cocaine explosion.

Webb spent more than a year uncovering the shady connection between the CIA and drug trafficking through the agency's relationship with the Nicaraguan contras, a right-wing army that aimed to overthrow the leftist Sandinista government during the 1980s. The Sandinistas were Marxist rebels who came to power in 1979 after the collapse of decades of U.S.-backed dictatorship at the hands of the Somoza family. President Reagan called the contras "freedom fighters" and compared them to America's founding fathers. Even as Reagan uttered those words, the CIA was aware that the many of the contras' supporters were deeply involved in cocaine smuggling, and were using the money to fund their army, or, as more often proved the case, to line their own pockets.

Many reporters had written about the CIA's collusion with contra drug smugglers, but nobody had ever discovered where those drugs ended up once they reached American soil. "Dark Alliance" provided the first dramatic answer to that mystery by profiling the relationship between a pair of contra sympathizers in California, Danilo Blandon and Norwin Meneses, and "Freeway" Ricky Ross, the most notorious crack dealer in the history of South Central's crack trade.

"Dark Alliance" created history in another way: it was the first major news exposé to be published simultaneously in print and on the Internet. Ignored by the mainstream media at first, the story nonetheless spread like wildfire through cyberspace and talk radio. It sparked angry protests around the country by African-Americans who had long suspected the government had allowed drugs into their communities. Their anger was fueled by the fact that

"Dark Alliance" didn't just show that the contras had supplied a major crack dealer with cocaine, or that the cash had been used to fund the CIA's army in Central America—but also strongly implied that this activity had been critical to the nationwide explosion of crack cocaine that had taken place in America during the 1980s.

It was an explosive charge, although a careful reading of the story showed that Webb had never actually stated that the CIA had intentionally started the crack epidemic. In fact, Webb never believed the CIA had conspired to addict anybody to drugs. Rather, he believed that the agency had known that the contras were dealing cocaine, and hadn't lifted a finger to stop them. He was right, and the controversy over "Dark Alliance"—which many consider to be the biggest media scandal of the 1990s—would ultimately force the CIA to admit it had lied for years about what it knew and when it knew it.

But by the time that happened, Webb's career as a journalist would be over. Just two months after his story appeared, the most powerful newspapers in the country had published massive rebuttals to "Dark Alliance." Webb increasingly became a focus of those attacks, as the mainstream media began digging through his twenty-year career, looking for evidence of bias that would bolster their attacks on his credibility. In less than a year, the *San Jose Mercury News* would back away from the story, forcing Webb to a tiny regional bureau of the paper. He quit his job and never worked for a major newspaper again.

The attacks continued even after Webb's death. The *L.A. Times* published an obituary that ran in newspapers across the country which summed up his life by claiming he was author of "discredited" stories about the CIA. The paper would later publish a lengthy feature story revealing that Webb had suffered from clinical depression for more than a decade—even before he wrote "Dark Alliance." Titled "Written in Pain," it painted Webb as a troubled, manic-depressive man who had repeatedly cheated on his wife, and a reckless "cowboy" of a journalist.

Such a portrait offers only a misleading caricature of a much more complicated man. Interviews with dozens of Webb's friends, family members and colleagues reveal that Webb was an idealistic, passionate, and meticulous journalist, not a cowboy. Those who knew him before "Dark Alliance" made him famous and then infamous say he was happy until he lost his career. His colleagues, with the exception of some reporters and editors at the *Mercury News* who found him arrogant and self-promoting, almost universally loved, respected and even revered him.

As this book will show, the controversy over "Dark Alliance" was the central event in Webb's life, and the critical element in his eventual depression and suicide. His big story, despite major flaws of hyperbole abetted and even encouraged by his editors, remains one of the most important works of investigative journalism in recent American history. The connection Webb uncovered between the CIA, the contras and L.A.'s crack trade was real—and radioactive. Webb was hardly the first American journalist to lose his job after taking on the country's most secretive government agency in print. Every serious reporter or politician that tried to unravel the connection between the CIA, the Nicaraguan contras and cocaine, had lived to regret it.

Senator John Kerry investigated it through congressional hearings that were stonewalled by the Reagan administration and for this, he was alternatively ridiculed and ignored in the media. Journalists like the AP's Bob Parry quit their jobs after being repeatedly shut down by their editors. Some reporters, working on the ground in Central America, had even been subjected to police harassment and death threats for pursuing it. Webb was simply the most widely and maliciously maligned of these reporters to literally die for the story.

The recent history of American journalism is full of media scandals, from the fabulist fabrications of *The New Republic's* Stephen Glass and the *New York Times'* Jayson Blair to Judith Miller's credulous and entirely discredited reporting on Saddam Hussein's nonexistent weapons of mass destruction for the *New York Times*, which helped pave the way for the U.S. invasion of Iraq. Webb, despite his stubborn refusal to admit his own errors, hardly deserves to be held in such company. What truly distinguishes his fate is his how he was abandoned by his own employer in the face of unprecedented and ferocious attacks by the nation's major newspapers, the likes of which had never been seen before or occurred since.

The controversy over "Dark Alliance" forced Webb from journalism and ultimately led him to take his own life. Besides Webb, however, nobody else lost a job over the story—nobody at the CIA certainly, and not even any of Webb's editors, who happily published his work only to back away from it under withering media attacks before getting on with their lives and receiving promotions. Gary Webb's tragic fate, and the role of America's most powerful newspapers in ending his career, raises an important question about American journalism in an era where much of the public perceives the fourth estate as an industry in decline, a feckless broadcaster of White House leaks with a penchant for sensationalized, consumer-driven tabloid sex scandals.

Webb spent two decades uncovering corruption at all levels of power, at the hands of public officials representing all ideological facets of the political spectrum. Indeed, his very fearlessness in taking on powerful institutions and officials was an ultimately fatal character trait that nonetheless embodies the very sort of journalistic ethic that should be rewarded and celebrated in any healthy democratic society. In 2002, Webb reflected on his fall from grace in the book *Into the Buzzsaw*, a compendium of first-person accounts by journalists whose controversial stories ultimately pushed them from their chosen profession. His words are worth remembering now more than ever.

"If we had met five years ago, you wouldn't have found a more staunch defender of the newspaper industry than me," Webb concluded. "And then I wrote some stories that made me realize how sadly misplaced my bliss had been. The reason I'd enjoyed such smooth sailing for so long hadn't been, as I'd assumed, because I was careful and diligent and good at my job . . . The truth was that, in all those years, I hadn't written anything important enough to suppress."

BORN ON AUGUST 31, 1955, at

the apex of America's post-war economic boom to a nomadic household centered on his father's career as a Marine Corps sergeant, Gary Webb enjoyed an adventuresome if peripatetic childhood as a military brat. His father, William Webb, served as a Navy frogman in the Korean War and almost perished from a mine explosion while swimming to a submarine after an operation above the 38th parallel. After recovering from his wounds, he returned to Korea, serving in the air wing. A few months after the war's end, he found himself at a restaurant in San Francisco, where he met his future wife Anita, an Italian-American who had followed her brother, then serving in the Coast Guard, from Brooklyn to California.

Because the Marine Corps didn't have an adequate hospital in Hawaii, Anita Webb gave birth to her first-born son alone at a military hospital in Corona, California. Two months later, Webb's father rejoined the family when he was transferred to El Toro Marine Corps Air Station in Orange County, California. The family lived in nearby Los Alamitos until 1957, shortly after Webb's younger brother Kurt was born, when Bill was transferred again, first to Florida, then North Carolina and finally to Huntington Beach, California. A year later, Bill got his orders to transfer to Hawaii, where he was attached to a radio battalion.

"Gary was a strange child," Anita says. "He was very serious. He had big eyes and kept looking and looking, but didn't talk. He was very peculiar. But once he started talking, it never stopped." When Webb was two years old, he told his mother he had a headache. "Oh Gary," she said. "You're a hypochondriac. When she explained what the word meant, it became Webb's favorite word. "He ran around telling anyone who would listen that he was a hypochondriac."

In Hawaii, she insists, Gary spent the happiest years of his life. "We found a nice house up in the hills in Kaneohe and the kids started playing with the Hawaiian kids. It was good for them. Bill and I were water lovers. We were always near the beach. And this stereotype of a Marine Corps father—forget about it. He was always playing with the kids, teaching them how to swim and bodysurf."

Now a lawyer who works for defense contractors in San Jose, Kurt Webb recalls one of he and Gary's favorite pastimes was collecting shells—not from the beach but the

Marine Corps gunnery range. "We had a lot of independence and would run around until evening, going to the beach, building tree forts, popping Portuguese man-o-wars or having snail fights."

"Gary was very sensitive," Anita says. "I remember my brother came to visit when we were in Hawaii and took the kids out to the beach. My brother walked along the ocean with them and told them stories about the man who lived in the ocean and all these fairy tales. And then he picked up this tiny blue plastic soldier and told them this story about how this soldier had conquered all these lands. Well, one day, I'm cleaning Gary's drawers years later when he was in college, and there's the soldier. Gary was very sensitive about these things."

While still in grade school, Gary showed early talent in what would later become a passion for poring over complex documents—the hallmark of a true investigative reporter. "One time, he went to the PX and bought a book on the stock market," Anita says. Soon thereafter, Webb began to read the business section of the newspaper each morning and built a spreadsheet for tracking stock prices. One day, he told his parents he wanted to purchase stock in the Xerox Corporation. "His father and I were totally stupid on stocks," Anita says. "We didn't have tons of money. And his father said, 'You can't: it costs a lot of money to go into the stock market.' And Gary never forgave his father because he said he could have made a lot of money from buying stock in Xerox. He was an amazing young man."

When Webb was in seventh grade, the family left Hawaii. By then, his father had spent twenty years in the military and was ready to retire. "We talked about it, and at first we wanted to move to California," Anita says. "But my mother said 'Don't move to California: they're smoking pot and doing all sorts of horrible things.' Haight-Ashbury was going on. It was the '60s. We made the decision that Indianapolis was a safe place to raise children."

The family moved to Lawrence, Indiana, just outside the city. There, Anita recalls, "little girls looked like little girls and not hookers." Their house was located in a good school district, and the real estate agent told the Webbs that local kids won more college scholarships there than students at any other district in the city. "It was a good decision," Anita says. "The boys got a great education."

In Indianapolis, Bill Webb found a job as a security guard at a hospital. Faded family photographs show a typical suburban nuclear family: Bill a patriarch of ramrod-straight military bearing, Anita, a cheerful, checkered-blouse housewife, and Gary and Kurt slouching mischievously in striped T-shirts and sunglasses. Although thousands of miles from the ocean, the family still spent vacations on the water, either on a houseboat they'd moor on the Indiana River or at a beach cottage at the Outer Banks in North Carolina. But the most important family time transpired around the dinner table, where politics were openly discussed.

Although Anita was a staunch Republican, Bill was a Democrat, and by the late 1960s, both were adamantly opposed to the Vietnam War. "We always listened to the news and discussed politics around the dinner table," Anita says. "In the beginning, my husband believed in the Domino Theory. Over time he changed. And even though I was a

Republican, I was against it. But Gary was always apolitical. During the Vietnam War, Gary used to sit there reading the newspaper. He was in the sixth grade, and he'd keep track of the body counts from the war. Gary kept a running calculation of how many Vietnamese died and one day he said 'Well, we've killed the whole of Vietnam."

At Lawrence Central High School, Gary and his brother drifted apart. "Every time we moved, we'd go off together and explore," Kurt says. "Prior to junior high, we always had the same friends and did things together in the neighborhood. But in high school we separated and had our own friends. We had sibling rivalry; it was our competitive nature. He'd beat me up sometimes, because he was bigger, but I got my revenge. Gary was a thickheaded individual. He always wanted things his way. He always used to read stuff and absorb it and have all this knowledge in his head. He could sit down and read and suck all this knowledge out of stuff."

"He was just a goofy guy," says Greg Wolf, a lifelong friend who first met Webb at Belzer Junior High. "He was a horny teenager like the rest of us. There was no soccer or ballet or any of that crap. We just rode our bicycles and sat around. He and I used to go down to Madison, Indiana, a little town on the Indiana River where I had an aunt and we'd shoot guns and camp out. One day we went to a river and there was a dock there with a bunch of houseboats. They were all empty because it was winter. He gets off the dock, goes on one of these boats and starts snooping inside. He wasn't going to steal anything, but property rights never occurred to him. He wasn't afraid of anything."

Another high school friend, Mike Crosby, recalls that

despite his later reputation as a leftist reporter, Webb loved shooting guns. "We'd camp out, a dozen of us, on this unimproved property down in Jefferson County, and shoot guns," he says. "Rifles, handguns, whatever people had. Gary would say, 'I'm not one of those anti-gun people. I'm a member of the Greenpeace Liberation Front. We shoot hunters.'"

Gary's fearlessness as a reporter surfaced in his first work of journalism, in a story that convinced him he had found his true calling. It was 1970, Richard Nixon was in the White House, the increasingly unpopular Vietnam War was still raging, but Webb wasn't out in the streets protesting. Given that his interests ranged from cars and bikes to guns and girls, it's not surprising that his first story combined guns and girls. In a 1999 speech in Eugene, Oregon, Webb recalled how he got his start in journalism with a piece he wrote for his school paper about the high school's militaristic cheerleading squad.

"I think I was fifteen," he said. "They thought it was a cool idea to dress women up in military uniforms and send them out there to twirl rifles and battle flags at halftime. And I thought this was sort of outrageous, and I wrote an editorial saying I thought it was one of the silliest things I'd ever seen. And my newspaper advisor called me the next day and said, 'Gosh, that editorial you wrote has really prompted a response.' And I said, 'Great, that's the idea, isn't it?' And she said, 'Well, it's not so great, they want you to apologize for it.'"

According to Webb, he refused to apologize. "They said, 'Look, why don't you just come down and the cheerleaders are going to come in, and they want to talk to you and tell you what they think,' and I said okay. So I went down to the newspaper office, and there were about fifteen of them sitting around this table, and they all went around one by one telling me what a scumbag I was, and what a terrible guy I was, and how I'd ruined their dates, ruined their complexions, and all sorts of things . . . and at that moment, I decided, 'Man, this is what I want to do for a living.'"

"I don't think you can attach any political weight to it," Wolf insists. On the one hand, Webb was serious about being a reporter. "He was delivering papers for the *Lawrence Journal*, and I guess he worked his way up there writing articles for them, too," he says. But Wolf says Webb was just screwing around with the drill team satire. "He wasn't a pacifist or anything like that," he says. "His dad was a Marine. Gary and I would go shoot guns. It wasn't a Birkenstock and Volvo kind of thing. I never thought it was a seminal event in Gary's writing career, but it was sort of typical of him. Gary wasn't afraid of anything. It was a sort of character flaw."

Kurt Webb says his brother found the whole experience hilarious. "I don't think he really apologized," he says. "He just said 'I'm sorry you were offended.' He had the attitude that it was their problem and if they didn't like it they could write something about him. Gary always had a flippant attitude about stuff like that, how people could get so uptight about such a simple little thing."

"It was a good piece," Anita Webb says. "I thought it was very funny." But when parents of the cheerleaders demanded an apology from Webb, she confronted his teacher. "I told her that if anyone should apologize, she should, because she was the one who submitted the essay to the paper," she says. "And Gary came home from school and said he got up in class and said he was sorry. Gary just felt it was the better thing to do. Everyone was just pouncing all over the poor kid."

WHEN WEBB GRADUATED from high school, he won a Hoosier scholarship and chose to attend IUPI, a community college whose initials stand for Indiana University/Purdue University in Indianapolis. "IUPI was where the poor kids went," says Rex Davenport, one of Webb's college friends who now edits a magazine for the Washington, D.C.-based American Society for Training and Development. At IUPI, Davenport edited the school newspaper, *The Sagamore*, where Webb wrote music reviews.

"He showed up as a freshman and started working for me," Davenport says. "We were an independent bunch and didn't have a lot of supervision. We didn't cover much hard news; it was all opinions and rants. I certainly didn't teach him anything, but Gary was a good critic. We got a lot of free vinyl, and a lot people hung out at the newspaper for the free records."

Davenport recalls that Webb mostly wrote about his favorite bands, Mott the Hoople and Roxy Music, but just as in high school, he also wrote scathing satires about campus events. When a liberal history professor sponsored an antiwar film series at the school, Webb helped pen several reviews of the series, each freighted with self-parodying pacifist clichés.

"We got irked because there was all this money being spent on a film series that was essentially just antiwar propaganda," Davenport says. "Not that any of us were against that necessarily, but it was horribly one-sided. The professor called the series 'Battle Cry of Peace,' and we just mocked it horribly. We kept running headlines like 'Battle Cry of Peace,' 'More Battle Cry of Peace,' and 'Still More Battle Cry.' Gary was on board for that. It was pretty funny considering that Gary was a military brat."

The lack of editorial supervision at *The Sagamore* meant that campus reporters had to police each other. "Some kid had written a film review and convinced us to run it, and I got called on the carpet because the kid had stolen it from *Playboy*," Davenport says. "Gary found him a day later and dragged him into a restaurant and threatened to beat him up, but didn't. He explained that we didn't want our reputation messed with that way. He had a sort of honest streak in him back then and always did. He just didn't suffer fools at all. If you weren't honest and straight-forward, he had no use for you at all."

In the summer of 1975, Webb got a job with *City Lights of Indianapolis*, a fledgling alternative weekly. His IUPI friend, Rex Davenport, was the paper's managing editor. "We were mostly focused on arts and entertainment," Davenport says. "Gary did some big interviews for us that summer: Billy Joel and maybe Paul McCartney." David Letterman, then a local celebrity weatherman, wrote a piece for the paper as well. Davenport can't recall what it was about, but wasn't impressed. "It made no sense," he says. "It was crap, actually."

Webb spent most of his free time hanging around with Greg Wolf, who often borrowed Gary's rebuilt MG, a blue roadster that he and his dad had picked up at a local junk-yard. With his father, Webb rebuilt the engine and repainted the car. His father fashioned a personalized brass plaque for the dashboard, which read, "This car built especially for Gary Webb."

Wolf was a year behind Webb in high school. Through a girlfriend, he met a beautiful brunette named Sue Bell. "I asked Sue out," he recalls. "It wasn't a big deal or anything. We were just friends, but Gary had the hots for her." On that first date, Wolf borrowed Webb's car.

Sue laughs when she recalls what went through her mind when she noticed the plaque. "I was sixteen," she says. "I thought 'My, he must have a lot of money.' Greg asked if I wanted to go back to his parent's house. Gary was there watching TV. He used to hang out there and watch old Godzilla movies and stuff and make fun of them and laugh. He was just sitting there. He talked to me a little, but he was really shy. But two weeks after that, he asked me out and we started dating. And two weeks after that he told me he was moving to Kentucky."

Bill Webb had found a new job in Cincinnati. Gary and Kurt gave up their scholarships and transferred to Northern Kentucky University. Webb spent the next four years there studying journalism, working for the school paper, *The Northerner*, and traveling back to Indianapolis to see Sue. "I figured we'd never see each other again, but somehow we made it work," she says.

Anita Webb says she realized her son was going to marry Sue the first time she saw them together. "They were in the dining room sitting near this big window," she says. "She was a sweet girl, very nice, and just sixteen at the time. He fell for her. They were always together. When we moved to Kentucky, I figured he'd get over it. But they kept communicating. The funny thing is, she would write him and he would take a red pen and correct her letters. I'd say 'Gary, you can't do that.' But she put up with him. I couldn't believe it. I would have ditched him right away. But he was funny that way. Very strange."

More than thirty years later, Sue still has those letters, including one from July 11,1974. "Your mistakes are getting fewer, thanks to my brilliant tutelage," Webb wrote. "Here they are: 'Sorry I haven't written sooner' should read 'Sorry I didn't write sooner.' The tense in your sentence doesn't agree." After pointing out several other grammatical errors, Webb added, "'Alex finally took Pam out from the bank' doesn't make any sense. (By the way, 'sense' is not spelled 'since.') Did he take her out from the bank or out for a date? (I knew what you meant but grammatically, it's wrong.)"

Webb then pointed out that "a lot" is not one word, "to often," is spelled "too often," and "No, you better not," should read, "No, you'd better not." "Don't get me wrong," he added. "I'm glad to get your letters and I want one a day if you manage. Well, enough corrections; let's get to the meat of your article."

According to Sue, those corrections, annoying as they were, also showed that her boyfriend couldn't stop thinking about her. Halfway through one of his letters to Sue, in fact, he realized he was in love. "Oh, shit," he wrote. "For once, I can't even think of the words to tell you. This is the first time words have ever failed me. Words were created by man to tell of happenings and not of inner feelings. They don't describe the emotions of the . . . deepest emotions I feel. And they shouldn't. What I feel for you is too delicate to be mauled by unwieldy words. A touch, a look, a sign between us is the proper medium."

When he was eighteen years old, Webb's parents separated and two years later, divorced. The experience damaged him in a way that left him unable to talk about it to anyone. "Gary was very intense and he kept a lot of emotions very tight to himself," Anita says. "A lot of the disappointments he had in life, he kept to himself."

Kurt Webb says his older brother never truly recovered from the divorce. "Gary was a strong sentimental family man," he says. "He took umbrage to our parents getting divorced. Gary was an idealist. He wanted a perfect world where people weren't corrupt and where family life really mattered."

Anita wouldn't say what led to the separation. "It was a stressful time," she says. "Things were up in the air. I don't remember. We got in an argument, and he said he was leaving and I said that was fine with me." But she added that her son never forgave his father for the divorce. "When his father broke away from the family, that bothered Gary a great deal," she says. "I didn't go into gross detail with the kids about why I didn't want to live with their father, because he was a very devoted father. He might not have been the best husband, but there's nobody who had a better father than those kids."

After his parent's divorce, Webb moved in with Sue's parents in Indianapolis. They were already talking about marriage. "My parents had a five bedroom house and said he could live with us," Sue recalls. "So he moved in for about a year, long enough for my dad to be not too happy about it."

Sue says Webb told her his father had been unfaithful. "He confronted his dad about it when he was eighteen years old," she says. "His father was a cheater and Gary was always pissed off about it. He asked him how he could do that. And his dad said, 'Oh Gary, you wait ten or fifteen years. Just imagine if you marry Sue and you're off in some other country and a beautiful woman approaches you in a bar. What are you going to do?' That's the answer he got from his father. Isn't that nice?"

Just shy of graduating from Northern Kentucky University, Webb quit school and started looking for a job. Across the river from Cincinnati was Covington, Kentucky, where Webb had heard from a friend that Vance Trimble, the eccentric, curmudgeonly editor of *The Kentucky Post*, had a reputation for hiring people off the street if they made a good first impression.

Sin City THREE

TOM LOFTUS STILL remembers seeing a handsome young man with a thin packet of clippings walk through the doors of the *Kentucky Post* one morning in early 1978. Now the state capital bureau chief for the *Louisville Courier-Journal*, Loftus was a young reporter at the Covington, Kentucky-based *Post* when Gary Webb asked to see Vance Trimble, the paper's editor.

"Someone had told him that the editor was always looking for people and if you went there early in the morning, you could get a job," Loftus says. "Vance was eccentric and mean, but a hell of a smart guy. He would hire people on a one-day basis."

Getting the job meant more than impressing Trimble in an interview. Loftus doesn't know for certain, but says

Trimble typically sent potential hires directly into the field to cover a breaking story. I'm pretty sure he told Gary, 'You look young, but go see the city editor and we'll put you to work,'" he says. "He probably went out on a trial basis to cover a traffic fatality on deadline."

In an April 1998 interview with author Charles Bowden, who profiled Webb that year for *Esquire* magazine in a feature story called "The Pariah," Webb recalled that Trimble told him to find two stories and report back to him in a week. He went home, sat in his back yard and thought it over. "Fuck, I can do this," he thought to himself. Webb went back to Trimble with a story about strippers in Newport, Kentucky, and a man who carved gravestones for a living. Trimble rejected the stripper story as a "twice-told tale," but liked Webb's writing enough to tell him to find two more stories. A week later, he gave Webb another week to find two more articles, and Webb realized that, despite feeling like he was on perpetual probation, he had started writing full-time.

Now retired and living in Oklahoma City, Trimble doesn't recall the details of how he came to hire Webb, but he still remembers him almost thirty years later. "He was green as grass but eager as hell," Trimble says. "He was bright and good-looking and wanted to write." Trimble says Webb called him years later, shortly after he published "Dark Alliance," to thank him for giving him his first job. "He was very emotional," Trimble says. "I don't know if he was about to cry, but he thanked me for five or ten minutes."

The *Kentucky Post* was located on the second floor of an office building where fifteen reporters cramped together like mechanics in a boiler room scrambled to assemble the paper every morning by 9:30 a.m. The paper consisted of sixteen pages wrapped around the *Cincinnati Post* and delivered every afternoon to 55,000 residents in suburban Cincinnati and a dozen rural counties in northern Kentucky. Covering the news often required driving more than 100 miles a day to compile arrest reports, hospital and jail admissions, lawsuit filings, and birth and death reports from small towns.

Any information that didn't pan out into a full story was dutifully transcribed into the paper's celebrated "Town Crier" section. "It wasn't a very glorious beginning for a reporter, going into a county clerk's office, plopping down a typewriter and checking all the lawsuits," Loftus says. "But you got a lot of stories that way. Good reporters are supposed to check that kind of thing."

Another obligation imposed by Trimble was covering high school football games. Every Friday night, six city desk reporters would receive marching orders to fan out to local games. A favorite pastime of reporters stuck with that assignment was to insert clichés into their work that Trimble would often overlook on deadline. For that reason, Webb grew to relish the assignment.

"Every time Gary covered a football game he'd check who had carried the ball for the most yardage," Loftus says. "And the third or fourth paragraph of every one of his stories would usually contain the phrase 'Johnny so-and-so carried the ball however many times, *grinding up the yardage like cheap hamburger.*' Gary would always howl when he got a good cliché in there, usually while he was smoking a cigarette behind his typewriter."

A former Washington, D.C.-based correspondent for the Scripps Howard news agency, Trimble had won numerous awards, including a 1961 Pulitzer Prize, for his reporting. He had forty years of experience in journalism, and liked to point that out whenever he called reporters into his office to berate their work. Trimble says he doesn't remember yelling at Webb, but guesses he did. "I yelled at everybody," he says.

Trimble says his reporters were always after the big scoop, but were often "as green as they were eager." One reporter called him at home late one evening, saying that he had been in a convenience store that appeared to be running a mob-tied bookie operation. "People were coming in and saying, 'Give me five dollars on number four, or three dollars on number two,'" the reporter told Trimble. "He wanted to call the police right away and have them raid the place," Trimble says. "I said, 'You damn well better not do that; we'll assess this in the morning.' Sure enough, it turned out the people were coming in there to buy gasoline."

"You didn't want to get called into his office," Loftus says. "If he walked out into the newsroom and pointed to you and said 'Get in here,' it was going to be a bad day to say the least. You knew you were going to get the speech, and the speech always had the same line: 'This is the worst piece of shit I have seen in forty years of journalism.' The problem was he was usually right."

Trimble wasn't especially fond of investigative reporting, but to him no story was too small for painstaking detail. He wanted every possible question in every story answered. After the paper had been sent to the printer each morning, reporters spread across northern Kentucky looking for news. They knew not to bother showing up the next morning without a well-developed and thoroughly researched story.

Although most of his staff regarded him as somewhat of a tyrant, Loftus says, they also recognized his genius. "There's no newspaper I can think of that was more cognizant of what was going on in its circulation area," Loftus says. "It had a lot of the qualities of a really good tabloid. Trimble was a brilliant guy, but he had some unique ideas and it was a weird newspaper. He loved tearjerker stories about missing or sick children."

Such stories inevitably earned darkly humorous unofficial headlines among *Post* staffers. "One story was the 'Little Blue Ricky' story," Loftus says. "Little Blue Ricky had some sort of heart condition which caused his complexion to fade and turn blue. Then there was 'Tiny Mark Stone.' Tiny Mark Stone was an infant who was lost by his mother and nobody could figure out where he was. Trimble couldn't get enough of that story."

A month after Tiny Mark Stone vanished, police located a dead baby that was almost certainly the missing infant. "But for some reason, maybe the advice of their lawyers, the parents never claimed the body," Loftus says. "And the police couldn't positively identify the baby because the body had deteriorated. We ran this story called 'Nobody Wants Dead Baby,' which for some reason strikes me as a really interesting headline when you think about it. Trimble told me to get out there and find out where they were going to bury this kid. I drove out to the county potter's field, this ugly patch of land out there somewhere and we ran this big picture and a caption, 'Baby To Be Buried Here.'"

After that particular story ran, dozens of telephone calls came into the newspaper from preachers and funeral directors, all offering their services. "Apparently, Tiny Mark Stone was buried in a proper burial service attended by no less than fifteen reporters and camera crews from every TV station in a fifty-mile radius," Loftus says.

Another famous—and among his reporters, infamous—Trimble story was "Major the Dog."

It all started when Tom Scheffey, then the *Post*'s statehouse reporter and now senior writer of the *Connecticut Law Tribune*, received a telephone call about a wounded canine. "I wrote this fairly short but heart-wrenching story about this injured puppy with no owner," he says. "A young woman who was an intern for us volunteered to take over the dog's care for a while. She came back and said we should put this dog out of its misery, but Vance picked up the phone and called a veterinarian and told him to make this dog live. Nobody thought it could be done, but Vance scared this surgeon into performing an operation."

Trimble assigned Webb to attend the surgery. His story on the operation ran on the front page and featured a photograph of him in the operating room, wearing a surgeon's mask. Major the Dog survived to be adopted by a little boy. "Gary called that story his 'claim to shame,'" Loftus says. "Everybody had some overplayed tearjerker story at that paper, and that was his."

Greg Wolf occasionally accompanied Webb on his assignments. He recalls Webb griping about covering traffic accidents or murders and having to interview recently bereaved family members, a task some *Post* staffers jokingly referred to as the "Good Morning Widow Jones. Well, You Are *Now*" beat. "He said his job was to go to the front door and ask the mother how it felt to have her son stabbed to death," Wolf says. "He did that once and the lady didn't know about it yet."

SHORTLY AFTER HE joined the *Kentucky Post*, Webb asked Sue to marry him. They were wed in a Unitarian ceremony in Indianapolis on February 10, 1979. "I remember Webb found a Unitarian Church," Wolf says. "He said he told the minister 'You can do whatever you want, but I don't want to hear you mention Jesus.'" The wedding reception took place at Wolf's bachelor pad. "We had spaghetti and wine," Wolf adds. "It was a lot of fun, the best wedding reception I've ever been to in my life."

After the wedding, Webb and his wife moved to a working-class neighborhood in Covington, Kentucky. "We lived in this place called Seminary Square, where people were trying to fix up these old homes," Sue says. At the time, she was pregnant with their first son, Ian, and Webb was understandably concerned about her safety. After a thief broke into his car and stole his radio, he rigged up an alarm that would ring inside the house when someone tried to open the car door. "One day it started beeping," Sue says. "Gary grabbed his rifle and this big black guy was pushing his car down the alley."

Webb confronted the man. Instead of running away, the would-be thief came toward him, turning away only as Webb pulled the trigger. Bleeding from his backside, the man tore down the alley on foot before passing out. Fortunately, he survived and was later convicted of trying to steal the car. "The neighbors got Gary a trophy," Sue says. "After that, everything calmed down much more in the neighborhood."

Scheffey remembers worrying that his friend might be charged in the shooting. "For a while it was thought they might bring Gary up on charges," he says. "A lot of defense lawyers said they'd defend him for free if the cops laid a finger on him." But the cops never charged Webb, who had a license for the gun and was acting in self-defense. "There's a big irony there," Scheffey says. "Gary was the darling of the black community after the 'Dark Alliance' story. But did anyone tell them about the incident where he shot a black guy in the ass?"

If Covington had its rough side, it had nothing on neighboring Newport, Kentucky. The city has cleaned up its image in the past twenty years, but in the early 1980s it was known among *Kentucky Post* reporters as "Sin City," a red-light district for Cincinnati that was known as a mafia town. Monmouth Street, Newport's main drag, teemed with porno shops, bars, and strip clubs, some of which were regular hangouts for *Post* staffers.

The town had a colorful, populist mayor known as Johnny "TV" Peluso, who owned a TV repair shop downtown. He was renowned for passing out quarters to kids in the street whenever an ice cream truck drove by. In the mid-1980s, Peluso went to federal prison for lying to a grand jury and pressuring city employees to misuse public funds.

Shortly after joining the paper, Scheffey says, his colleagues brought him to a Newport club called the Pink Pussy Cat. "There was a dancer there named Savage Sheena and she needed a volunteer she could go after with her bull whip," he says. "I was twenty-five and clean cut and obviously not a plant and she took me out of the audience. I don't know what I was doing with a cigarette because I had quit, but she took that cigarette out of my lip from twenty-five feet away without splitting my nose."

"It was like Vegas, a wild-ass town," recalls Wolf, adding that he used to visit Newport with Webb when his friend was on assignment there. His favorite hangout was a strip club called the Brass Ass. "There was a juke box on the stage, the girls would come out and put a quarter in the box and dance completely nude," he says. "It was like watching a gynecological exam from two feet away. Then they'd try to get you to buy a bottle of champagne. Gary interviewed a lot of those strippers. He got to be very popular with them."

EARLY IN HIS job at the *Kentucky Post*, while covering the police beat in Newport, Webb came across the story that would launch his career as an investigative reporter. On a cold January night in 1978 an unknown assailant walked into an adult bookstore on Monmouth Street, took out a handgun and shot the proprietor, Lester Lee, who died from his wounds at a local hospital. When police searched his pockets, they found a wallet full of business cards, several of which belonged to businessmen connected to the coal industry, and one bearing the name of a State Senator in Ohio.

Scheffey, who had just started studying law, told Webb he'd help him with the story. "I worked with him on some of the early stories," Scheffey says. "But Gary did the lion's share of the work. Gary was just enthralled with it. He traced down Lester Lee's story."

Webb quickly discovered that Lee wasn't just an ordinary porn merchant; he was a reputed mobster who had been on the FBI's ten most wanted list. Lee was also the president of a coal company that didn't seem to have any other employees.

"Lee was basically a con man looking for the next big scam," Scheffey says. "He wanted to be a big shot. Previously, he had been in speculative stocks, but then he capitalized on the oil crisis." As Webb and Scheffey discovered, nations without their own oil industry were scrambling to get fuel sources. "Lee realized if you had a corrupt minerals engineer, you could send them proof you had a boatload of coal, get a letter of credit, and cash it before they realized it was a bunch of dirt," he says. "That's why Lee died: the people who knew what he was up to caught up with him."

Webb and Scheffey drove north to the state capitol in Columbus, Ohio, and interviewed State Senator Donald "Buz" Lukens, the politician whose business card had been found in Lee's pocket. Lukens, a Republican party activist, had been the Midwest campaign coordinator for Ronald Reagan's first presidential race in 1976. He didn't deny his relationship with Lee. It wouldn't have been convincing if he had, however: Webb and Scheffey confronted him with a photograph of himself, Lee, and Reagan getting off an airplane during a campaign stop.

"Lukens thought it was just fine to be doing business with Lester Lee," Scheffey says. "Lee was his business associate, partner, friend, and resource. Lee wanted to impress Lukens and got him this plane. The plane was used in a five-state swing that essentially launched Reagan's first presidential bid." Scheffey went to Washington, D.C., and asked some questions at the Federal Elections Commission. "You have to report donations of that type of value, and they didn't," he says.

Lee's murder—and his ties to Lukens and Reagan—formed the basis for what eventually became a goliath seventeen-part series that Webb and Scheffey authored together called, "The Coal Connection."

"Vance [Trimble] was not crazy about the idea," Scheffey recalls. "He said, 'Webb, your trench coat is flapping in the wind.' Trimble discouraged Gary because he felt it was a disjointed international story, but he was doing what almost all editors do: they don't let excited young reporters take months and months or weeks or even unaccountable days to do complex investigative journalism."

Webb didn't press his case with Trimble. Instead, he and Scheffey worked on the story in their free time for the next two years. The *Kentucky Post* finally ran the story in 1980, shortly after Trimble retired from journalism. The series had three major parts. The first focused on Lee, his coal credit scam, and his relationship to Lukens. The second exposed the fact that Kentucky was the only state in the country where heavy equipment used in coal mining wasn't registered. As a result of the relative lack of paperwork attached to the vehicles, Webb and Scheffey discovered, it was easy to export stolen tractors to other countries. The pair even discovered evidence that some of the vehicles had been shipped by organized crime syndicates to South America as collateral for major cocaine deals.

Sheffey now feels that the drug dealing was rather tangential to the basic story they were trying to tell, but thanks to his colleague's passion for detail, "The Coal Connection" marked Webb's first journalistic venture into not only organized crime, but Latin America's booming cocaine trade. To get that part of the story, the two reporters drove out to a federal prison in Ashland, Kentucky and interviewed a colorful crook named J. R. Durham about the black market in mining equipment. On the way there, Scheffey's car broke down. "Gary got out and fixed the problem in five minutes," Scheffey says. The interview was worth the trip. "Durham was just laughing up his sleeve about all the people he had ripped off."

The third series of articles in "The Coal Connection" exposed how President Richard Nixon had created a tax incentive for coal companies to write off losses. "The tax scam people were quick to realize that if you funded a business with advance royalties, and then your company goes bust, the IRS would let you write off the loss on a dollar-for-dollar credit," Scheffey says. "It was a very powerful tax shelter, and there were all these doctors and mafia-tied individuals and companies who were funding them and getting all these tax benefits."

When Reagan came through the Midwest on his 1980 presidential campaign, Webb and Scheffey dogged his campaign throughout Ohio, trying to ask the candidate about his relationship with Lukens. They never got the interview. According to Scheffey, Reagan's campaign spokesman quit rather than answer Webb's questions.

Lukens went on to become a U.S. Congressman in

1986. Three years later, an Ohio television station filmed him at a McDonald's restaurant talking with the mother of a sixteen-year-old African-American girl whom Lukens had paid for sexual favors. He pled guilty to contributing to the delinquency of a minor, spent thirty days in jail, but refused to give up his seat. The following year, an elevator operator at the U.S. capitol building accused him of fondling her. In 1995, Lukens was convicted of five counts of bribery and conspiracy and sentenced to thirty months in federal prison.

After the series ran, the *Kentucky Post* submitted "The Coal Connection" for a Pulitzer Prize. It didn't win one, but did receive the 1980 Investigative Reporters & Editors award. Scheffey and Webb flew to San Diego with their wives to accept the award. "The *New Republic* featured our series on their back page, so they must have thought it was significant," Scheffey says. "But that was it. It wasn't the last time Gary's stories didn't catch on in the major media."

One journalist who did catch on to Webb's work was Walt Bogdanich, an investigative reporter at the *Cleveland Plain Dealer* who went on to work for *60 Minutes*, the *Wall Street Journal* and the *New York Times*. Bogdanich was investigating the Beverly Hills Supper Club in Northern Kentucky, which he described as "an illegal gambling house run by old-line mob people," some of whom were in Cleveland. While talking to other reporters about the story, one of them recommended he contact Webb, who had just written a great exposé on the Kentucky mafia.

Bogdanich says he was immediately drawn to Webb. "He was a very funny guy," he says. "He had this very cynical sense of humor which I share. I found him to be a delight to be around. I made it my job to try to get him to come to the *Plain Dealer*."

FOUR

The Big One

IF THE *KENTUCKY POST* is where Gary Webb learned how to become an investigative reporter, it was at the *Cleveland Plain Dealer* where he truly blossomed. Webb arrived at the 500,000-circulation daily—one of the largest and most venerable newspapers in the Midwest—in 1983. Coming from a small-town daily paper to a regional powerhouse was no small achievement, but Webb didn't get the job just because he had an insider like the *Plain Dealer*'s Walt Bogdanich on his side.

With five years of daily reporting experience and an award-winning investigative series on his resume, Webb won the job purely on his own merits, says Bogdanich, now an editor at the *New York Times*. New hires had to share computer terminals, and Webb's computer buddy was Tom

Andrzejewski, a thirty-five-year-old Clevelander who had joined the paper as a copyboy fresh from high school, working his way up the ranks to a reporter desk deep inside the newsroom, in a cramped corner known as the "quadrant."

Webb would later write about Andrzejewski in the introduction to his 1998 book, *Dark Alliance*, although not by name. "I was assigned to share a computer terminal with a tall, middle-aged reporter with a long, virtually unpronounceable Polish name," Webb wrote. "To save time, people called him Tom A."

Andrzejewski, Webb recalled, liked to curse. Instead of saying "yes," in answer to a question, he said, "fuckin'-a-tweetie." He referred to recalcitrant public officials and editors he didn't like as "fuckin' jerks." But what Webb remembered most about Andrzejewski was how he answered the phone. He would point at it, wink at Webb with facetious intuition and declare, "It's the Big One."

"No matter how many times I heard that, I always laughed," Webb wrote. "The Big One was the reporter's holy grail—the tip that led you from the daily morass of press conferences and cop calls on to the trail of The Biggest Story You'd Ever Write, the one that would turn the rest of your career into an anticlimax."

Now president of The Oppidan Group, a Cleveland public relations firm, Andrzejewski fondly remembers Webb as a Jeff Foxworthy look-alike who constantly talked about sports cars and motorcycles with the paper's auto reporter, who once gave Webb a bubble-wrapped engine part as a prank gift. The joke was that the part belonged to a Buick—the last type of car in the world Webb would ever drive.

"Gary was a hotshot investigative reporter," Andrzejewski says. "But he was also really fun. He had a great sense of humor in a very classic journalist skepticism-bordering-on-cynicism kind of way." Webb also had his serious side. "He was an honest industrious guy, but with an edge, especially when it came to exposing corrupt public officials or inept government agencies."

Another denizen of the quadrant was Steve Luttner. Recruited from the *Columbus Citizen Journal*, he was one of about a dozen reporters, including Webb, who were hired by the *Plain Dealer* to beef up investigative coverage of state government. Still a reporter at the paper's Columbus bureau, Luttner recalls the paper's 1950s-era Cleveland newsroom as the journalistic equivalent of a third world sweatshop.

"It was a dump," Luttner says. "It had an open floor and no air circulation and people smoked in there. Gary sat behind me for a year and a half." Luttner recalls Webb as a hard worker who was constantly on the telephone, chasing story leads. "He used to say that the system rewards persistence," he recalls. "Gary was always looking for targets. He would lock on to something and not let it go."

If Webb wasn't at his desk, he was in the law library researching cases and government codes, which he would then angrily recite chapter and verse in conversations with any official who refused to cooperate with him. "He would bludgeon people at agencies if he was getting any resistance from them," Luttner says. "I've never seen a more dogged reporter in thirty years."

Not everybody in the newsroom appreciated Webb's intensity or his perceived self-righteous approach to his job.

Webb could seem preachy when he ranted about crooked politicians. His view of ethics was black and white; there was no excuse for breaking the law, however obscure, and it was his mission as a reporter to expose such injustices, no matter how petty or technical. "I agreed with him," Luttner says. "But he could be a little uppity about that. I figured it was because he was the son of a Marine sergeant."

Now a doctoral candidate at Ohio University who left journalism six years ago, Tom Suddes had been at the *Plain Dealer* for just over a year when Webb arrived. "He had an in-your-face spirit of journalism," Suddes says. "He felt we weren't here to nurture people, we were here to raise hell, and I shared that view."

Webb often came to Suddes, who was known as a bipedal encyclopedia of Ohio politics, for advice on researching his stories. "One of Gary's great qualities as a reporter was that he had a great ability to pick brains," Suddes says. "He was never afraid to ask for guidance on how to find information. He was wonderful about ferreting out documents."

According to Suddes, Webb wasn't as straight-laced as other reporters. He had a Metallica sticker on his computer and liked to blast heavy-metal music from a tape deck while typing up his stories. Webb also enjoyed pulling pranks on his colleagues. There was an aquarium in the newsroom, and when one of the goldfish died, he and another reporter fished it out of the tank, wrapped it in some tissue paper and surreptitiously put it in the mailbox of a journalist at a competing paper who was digging into Cleveland's organized crime syndicates. The fish bore an ominous mafia-style warning: "Back Off."

Much of Webb's early reporting at the *Plain Dealer* involved improprieties at the state medical board. Walt Bogdanich had already written a series about the medical board. Webb picked up where he left off, exposing cronyism in the organization and, more importantly, the board's routine refusal to discipline doctors. Through public records requests, Webb obtained complaints from patients and tracked the board's failure to adequately investigate them.

Greg Wolf remembers Webb telling him about some of the more egregious cases where the medical board failed to discipline errant doctors. Webb got the address for a physician who he discovered was prescribing more diet pills than any other doctor in the country. The doctor ran a clinic out of his house that was open twice a week. Webb drove there, and saw a line of people waiting outside. Webb weighed only 160 pounds, but it was wintertime, and Webb wore several layers underneath a bulky winter jacket. When he got to the front of the line, the doctor asked him what was wrong.

"I'm fat," Webb responded. The doctor didn't ask him to take his coat off, but put him on a scale and gave him a bottle of pills. Webb returned two days later. "What do you want?" the doctor inquired. "More pills," Webb said. "What happened to the other pills I gave you?" the doctor asked. Webb wasn't counting on being recognized. He shrugged helplessly. "I had a party," he said.

As Webb told Wolf, the doctor asked no further questions and simply gave him another prescription. Another doctor Webb investigated was rumored to be mentally unstable. "Gary went out to her house and she was out in the garage with a hose, washing down the floor, and it was already immaculately clean," Wolf says. "He asked her what she was doing and she said, 'I am sluicing away the poison.'"

Apparently the doctor believed her contractor was trying to kill her. To prove it, she pointed at her car, which was splattered with mud stains. "The bombs! The bombs!" she said. "She thought the mud stains on her car were from bombs," Wolf says. "She was nuts and the medical board knew it and didn't do anything."

In 1984, Webb teamed up with Bogdanich to uncover a conflict of interest scandal at the Cleveland-Cuyahoga Port Authority. Cleveland sits on Lake Eerie; its docks unloaded shipping containers that came in through the Great Lakes from all over the world. All those containers needed insurance. A former school board president named Arnold Pinckney sat on the board of directors of the Port Authority. Pinckney also ran an insurance company and had sold $2 million worth of insurance to the Port Authority.

Pinckney had recently been appointed campaign manager for Jesse Jackson's first presidential bid. His lawyers held a press conference to denounce the article as "woefully incomplete" and full of factual errors. The *Plain Dealer* refused to retract the story. "He was indicted and convicted, then pardoned, because he was such a popular guy," Bogdanich says.

The Port Authority story was the first and last time Bogdanich collaborated with Webb. "He went off in his direction and I went in mine," he says. "We were both pretty strong-willed people." Bogdanich recalls arguing with Webb over certain details of a follow-up story Webb planned to write about Pinckney. "I thought he was too certain of a particular fact," he says. "He came to a conclusion that I didn't agree with. I just walked away, saying, 'Gary, It's your story.' It was a minor fact, but it showed how strong-willed he was."

Shortly after the Port Authority story ran, Bogdanich was transferred to the Columbus bureau of the *Plain Dealer*. Webb followed soon after, and they remained friends.

Bogdanich recalls going over to Webb's house frequently for dinner or to watch a movie. Webb's favorite film was *Caddyshack*.

"To understand Gary, you have to appreciate that Rodney Dangerfield character, this boisterous guy throwing around tip money in a country club," Bogdanich says. "Webb didn't suffer fools gladly, or people who were pompous, although some people criticized Gary for being that way himself."

One night, while sitting at a bar in Columbus, the two paid tribute to Dangerfield by creating a public nuisance in a stuffy setting. "This bar was where all the lobbyists hung out," Bogdanich says. "We got roaring drunk and started talking loudly about how we were going to buy a bunch of state senators. We just figured that's what people talked about in that place. We laughed so hard we had tears streaming down our faces."

In the summer of 1984, Bogdanich got a job at the *Wall Street Journal*. One of his easier assignments there was covering a golf tournament, which happened to be near Columbus. He rang up Webb. All he had to do was show up on time, and write a light, humorous piece about how golf writers had the easiest job in the world. It wasn't as easy as he thought. "I was doing a story about golf writers not putting in any hours and drinking too much beer," Bogdanich recalls. "It was a bit ironic, because Gary and I got so damn drunk that day I showed up late to the golf tent."

Just before Bogdanich departed for the *Wall Street Journal*, he tagged along with Webb for a few interviews on a story involving the Budweiser Cleveland Grand Prix, a charity auto race at Cleveland's Burke Lakefront Airport. In an article titled "Driving Off With the Profits," Webb reported that the race's promoters paid themselves nearly $1 million from money that should have gone to the city, an apparent violation of their lease. The promoter sued the *Plain Dealer* for libel. The case dragged on for years—long after Webb left the paper. Although none of Webb's facts were ever proven incorrect, the headline had implied more wrongdoing than the story had actually reported—a flaw that would come back to haunt Webb with his "Dark Alliance" story. A jury eventually awarded the plaintiffs $13.6 million.

Because he had accompanied Webb on the interviews, Bogdanich almost had to testify against his friend in court. "They were trying to get me to weigh in on my definition of the word 'profit,' " he says. "They tried to turn me against Gary, and it didn't work. I think the judge made some questionable rulings in that case. I know Gary was upset when the lawyers settled. He felt it could have been won on appeal."

Years later, after Webb published "Dark Alliance," the *New York Times* cited this settlement as evidence that Webb was a loose cannon prone to getting his facts wrong. But Gary Clark, then the *Plain Dealer's* managing editor and now managing editor for the *Denver Post*, says the paper never retracted the story because none of the facts were wrong, and all them came directly from public records. "The reporting was fine," Clark says. "The issue was a question of revenues

versus profits, which was clear in the story, but not the headline. To shoulder Gary with the blame would be unfair."

NOBODY AT THE *Plain Dealer* worked closer with Webb than
Mary Anne Sharkey. As a reporter with the now-defunct
Dayton Journal Herald in the early 1980s, she had read
Webb's series on corruption in the coal industry for the
Kentucky Post and was impressed enough to follow up on the
story. She confronted Donald "Buz" Lukens about his alleged
ties to the deceased mob figure Lester Lee. Lukens denied
everything and tried to pressure Sharkey not to write her
story. He failed. "Gary once told me I was the only journalist in the entire country to follow up on the Coal Connection," Sharkey says.

When Webb transferred to the Columbus bureau from
the *Plain Dealer*'s headquarters in Cleveland, Sharkey had
been at the paper for two years and had been promoted to
bureau chief. She had just finished an investigative series on
conflicts of interest surrounding Ohio State University's
medical school. The school's dean had a private practice
operating out the school, which gave him a handsome profit,
especially because his expenses, including his employees'
salaries, were paid for by state taxpayers.

Webb had just finished his exposé on the state medical
board when he got a call from the city coroner in Quincy, Illinois. The coroner told Webb to look into a doctor named
Michael Swango, a blond, blue-eyed paramedic who the
coroner believed had poisoned half a dozen of his colleagues

at an ambulance company in Quincy after being kicked out of Ohio State University's medical school. On several occasions, Swango had offered coffee and doughnuts to his co-workers, all of whom had experienced painful bouts of nausea and dizziness after consuming them. "Gary called me because I had done all this work on Ohio State University," Sharkey recalls.

She and Webb collaborated in an extensive investigation of Swango's tenure as an internist at Ohio State University's medical school. Between Webb's sources at the state medical board and Sharkey's contacts at the university, they discovered that both institutions had suspected Swango of killing several patients at the medical school's hospital, but instead of telling anyone, had simply covered it up to avoid bad publicity and lawsuits from the relatives of the patients who had died. "Gary was one of the most meticulous and dogged investigators," Sharkey says. "I'd come in the office, and he'd been in there all night, reading documents. We were breaking stories that ran on the national wires. If the medical school and the state medical board had done their jobs, Swango wouldn't have gone on to kill so many people."

After being convicted of seven counts of aggravated battery for poisoning his colleagues, Swango spent five years in an Illinois prison. He bounced around the country under a false name, leaving dead patients in his wake, before ultimately finding a job at a clinic in Zimbabwe. He was finally arrested in 1997, when his flight from Africa to Saudi Arabia made a stop in Chicago. After a 2000 trial, a Virginia jury sentenced Swango to life in prison for fatally poisoning three patients there years earlier.

Webb would later tell Sharkey they should have written a book about Swango. "It was one of our biggest regrets that we never did that," she says. "But Webb was first and foremost a journalist. He was interested in writing news stories. He just couldn't conceive of a life outside journalism."

One story Sharkey had to keep away from was a 1986 article Webb wrote entitled, "Mob-Linked Groups Donate To Chief Justice," an exposé of Cleveland lawyer Frank Celebrezze. Webb obtained a list of contributions to Celebrezze's Ohio Supreme Court campaign from a Cleveland laborer's union with ties to organized crime. "Most of the union's officers had been arrested and convicted or tied by an FBI indictment to the mob," Sharkey says.

Sharkey had written about Celebrezze before, so the *Plain Dealer*'s lawyers told her she couldn't help Webb with the story. After Celebrezze lost his re-election bid in a defeat widely attributed to Webb's reporting, he demanded a retraction. Webb's editors refused. Celebrezze sued the paper and won an undisclosed out of court settlement, which—along with the previous settlement over Webb's story on the charity racetrack—would later be cited by the *New York Times* as evidence that Webb was a bad reporter.

But just as with the racetrack story, Webb's colleagues recall that the settlement ultimately came down to the story's headline, not the reporting. "The story was carefully constructed," Sharkey says. "The headline is actually what made them settle the case."

The settlement marked the second time Webb's reporting had cost his employer dearly. While his colleagues regarded him as an especially aggressive reporter, they reject the assertions that followed in the wake of "Dark Alliance" that Webb was particularly prone to lawsuits. Hard-hitting investigative reporters are supposed to get sued, he often remarked—that's how you know you're doing your job. But given that the facts of his stories weren't proven wrong, Webb, for his part, felt betrayed by the settlement.

Webb and Sharkey continued to collaborate, with Webb doing the bulk of the reporting and investigative work, and Sharkey helping him by writing leads and shaping the copy. Occasionally, they would argue over the wording of a story, usually when Webb had inserted an over-the-top remark about a public official's apparent culpability high up in the piece. Webb respected Sharkey's abilities as an editor. He'd push her as far as he could, but would back off when she refused to cave in to his pressure.

"Gary was a challenging person to work with," Sharkey says. "But he was worth it. Sometimes you have a racehorse you have to flog to the finish line and sometimes you have a horse you have to pull the reins on. Gary was a reporter who needed you to pull the reins."

Together, they wrote several articles probing the extra-marital activities of Columbus mayor Dana Rinehart, who was being probed by a grand jury for allegedly performing cunnilingus on his fifteen-year-old babysitter. Although the police had closed the case without pressing charges, Webb filed a public records act request and got access to the case file. One of their stories revealed that while the babysitter had passed a police polygraph examination, Rinehart only agreed to take a test administered by his own expert.

The grand jury declined to indict Rinehart, but his

behavior eventually caught up with him. In 1990, he admitted lying about an affair with a married woman, and chose not to run for re-election. Six years later, Rinehart was arrested for drunk driving and leaving the scene of an accident after slamming into the rear of a police cruiser.

One of the funniest pieces Webb ever wrote was essentially a photo essay, Sharkey recalls. Webb compiled a list of people who worked for Ohio Governor Dick Celeste and checked property records to see what homes they owned before and after Celeste took office. "It was just a pictorial," Sharkey says. "But it was really funny. All these guys—from his campaign manager and communications person to his deputy chief of staff and cabinet members—lived in really modest houses and then moved into these big mansions after the election."

Gary had a "wonderful sense of humor," Sharkey adds. "He would get so tickled by these crooks. He would always be laughing really hard when we nailed one of them. He relished the showdown interview. He'd say, 'Now we have to publish their lies.' One of the ways people would harass each other in Columbus was by saying that Gary Webb of the *Plain Dealer* wants to interview you. It was a way of giving people heartburn."

Their collaboration ended in 1988 when Sharkey took a job in Cleveland as an editorial writer with the *Plain Dealer*. Webb wanted to succeed her as the Columbus bureau chief. But Gary Clark, the paper's managing editor, didn't think he'd fit that role. Neither did Sharkey. "I just didn't see him doing all the administrative work that needed to be done," she says. As it turned out, the person chosen to fill the position was widely regarded as a grossly unqualified editor. Webb told Sharkey he'd quit his job before working for her replacement. She tried to convince him to wait it out, but Webb refused.

"I will not work for him," Sharkey says Webb told her. "He's a fucking imbecile." Andrzejewski and other reporters at the paper agreed with Webb's assessment. "The *Plain Dealer* had a knack for attracting some of the most draconian and in some cases, just plain dumb editors," he says. "That was a major failing of the paper. Gary was a gem they should have tried to keep. Why he left the paper is a complicated thing, but having editors who were totally inept didn't help."

Leaving the *Plain Dealer* became an even more attractive idea when Webb got a call from a recruiter with the Knight Ridder News Service, who asked if he might be interested in moving to California. The *San Jose Mercury News* needed a qualified investigative reporter. Webb told the recruiter he couldn't afford to live in San Jose, but if they were willing to let him work in Sacramento, he'd be happy to cover state government. He told his editors at the *Plain Dealer* about the offer, and they begged him to stay, even offering a raise.

Sue figured her husband would stay put. The *Plain Dealer* was scrambling to keep her husband happy and he seemed surprised, even touched, by the effort. They had a four-year-old son, Ian, an infant named Eric; they liked their neighborhood and enjoyed a tight-knit group of friends at the paper. But one evening, Webb came home from work and told Sue he had accepted the job with the *Mercury News*. In response, the *Plain Dealer* had angrily given him one day to move out of his office before they changed the locks on the door to the Columbus bureau. "Gary said we were moving to California," Sue says. "And that was that."

UNDER THE TERMS of his hiring, Webb didn't have to pay his daily reporting dues at the *Mercury News* headquarters in San Jose, the typical procedure for new reporters before being promoted to more advanced assignments. Instead, he went straight to the paper's tiny Sacramento bureau, which at the time included only one other person. Because Webb had free reign to choose his targets, and wasn't required to do file daily stories, some people at the paper immediately resented the hotshot reporter from out of state. "Gary did not want to do bullshit," says Pamela Kramer, a former *Mercury News* reporter. "He was not quiet about not wanting to do bullshit. He could be arrogant. He had no problem with letting other people do the dailies."

One of Webb's later colleagues at the Sacramento bureau, Mitch Benson, now a public relations officer for University of California, Davis, refused to be interviewed for this book. But Bert Robinson, now an assistant managing editor for the *Mercury News*, had been working at the Sacramento bureau for a year when Webb arrived. He says he immediately liked Webb. "I was just happy to see a warm body, and to have somebody to talk to," he says. "Gary and I hit it off great. I went over to his house to watch ice hockey and smoke dope on weekends."

According to Robinson, he and Webb were also passionate music fans and used to see concerts and make mix tapes for each other. Webb, he recalls, was a huge Mott the

Hoople fan, and thought the band's lead singer, Ian Hunter, "walked on water." Robinson had more eclectic tastes in music and tried to turn Webb on to classic reggae artists like Toots and the Maytals, while Webb exposed him to California punk rock groups like Rancid and Offspring, which Robinson thought was a bit odd for a married guy in his late thirties.

At the bureau, Robinson covered the state budget, the governor's office, and the legislature, a heavy load for one reporter. Gary didn't seem to work nearly as hard. "Anyone who worked around him remarked on it," Robinson says. When Webb was chasing after a story, he gave it his full attention. But in between projects, he tended to show up late and leave early. He wanted to spend time with his two kids and never seemed to stop fixing up his house. "Gary loved to work on his house," Robinson adds. "When he came in each morning, he had been up all night working on the tile floor or redoing the wood trim in his bedroom."

"At the time, I really looked up to Gary as a hard-hitting investigative reporter," says Chris Knap, an *Orange County Register* reporter who then worked down the hall from Webb at the *Register*'s statehouse bureau. "I remember seeing him in his office. He never answered his phone: he just checked messages. He just worked on his own stories and ignored what the pack was doing. You'd never see him at a press conference. I think that caused some friction with other reporters. Occasionally I'd see him at one and I got the sense he had been ordered to get his ass out there."

A Midwesterner like Webb, Knap hails from West Virginia. Both men sported anachronistic moustaches and shared an enthusiasm for fast motorcycles and cars. "Gary was always a renegade," Knap says. "He always drove this Toyota Supra or some other pseudo sports car that still had his Ohio plates. He kept them on for years, which is a violation of the California vehicle code. A cop finally pulled him over for speeding and cited him for not having valid plates. Gary took the case to court and got the charge for the invalid plates dismissed because the cop couldn't prove how long he had been living here."

In the wake of the 1989 Loma Prieta earthquake, Webb teamed up with Pete Carey, a veteran correspondent for the *Mercury News* who had won a Pulitzer Prize for his joint coverage of the 1985 downfall of Filipino dictator Ferdinand Marcos. Together, Carey and Webb exposed how bureaucratic delays in retrofitting local "highways" had contributed to the earthquake disaster. Their work helped result in the paper's Pulitzer prize for team reporting that year.

Together with Robinson, Webb reported that California Governor Pete Wilson had vetoed legislation that would have harmed companies who had contributed to his campaign. They also teamed up on a story about Dom Cortese, a Democratic Assemblyman from San Jose. An anonymous tipster claimed that Cortese had carried a bill on behalf of the Painting & Decorating Contractors of California. In return, the source said, the group had given Cortese a free paint job for his house. But the group forgot to tell the contractor who did the work that it was a freebie. Ultimately, Cortese paid the contractor, but got his money back when he received an honorary fee from the group for a speech on painter's retirement funds.

Robinson and Webb figured if they called the contractor who had painted Cortese's house, word would reach the politician in time for him to come up with an explanation. So Robinson interviewed the contractor while Webb interviewed Cortese. "The contractor spilled, Gary got his interview, and we wrote the story," Robinson says. That was the highlight of their collaboration. Webb regaled his former colleagues at the *Plain Dealer* with the story, concluding that California politicians were guppies compared to their Midwestern counterparts when it came to graft. "It was the most fun we had," Robinson says. "The only thing I like better than corruption is completely inept corruption."

During their time together, adds Robinson, Webb displayed an amazing talent for working with documents. "It just seemed like a gift," he says. "He could pick up a 200-page report and skim through it and focus on one sentence on page 63 that suggested some huge outrage. If there was something buried in a document, I would miss it and Gary would always find it. It was amazing to watch. He was a hell of a reporter."

Another quality Webb had that distinguished him from other reporters was his crusading tendency to see the world in Manichean moral terms. "He quickly focused on who the good guys and bad guys were in a story," Robinson says. "He did not spend a lot of time doubting his conclusions. I think that it can be argued, in retrospect, that he took that to an extreme." Webb also professed more cynicism about editors than most reporters. He told Robinson that at the *Plain Dealer*, he had to take his files into his editor's office and defend every sentence.

To Webb, *Mercury News* editors appeared far less demanding; they seemed to do little more than check his story structure and spelling. "Webb was probably exaggerating," Robinson says. "But what strikes me in retrospect, is that if you are forged as a reporter in an adversarial editing setting, if you are used to your editors reining you in and ratcheting you back, you probably push things as far as you can."

One of the *Mercury News* editors who hired Webb, Scott Herhold, also supervised his work at the Sacramento bureau. He grew to regret it, saying that if he knew Webb had been sued at the *Plain Dealer*, he wouldn't have hired him. "I didn't know about the lawsuits," he says. "We didn't ask and he didn't tell us. We probably didn't do our due diligence on the problems he had there."

"I actually didn't like Gary that much," Herhold adds. "He was a very nasty guy." Herhold recalls that when the paper's management asked him to bring down the length of news stories, he wrote a memo to his writers asking them to cooperate, and Webb wrote a "long, nasty letter" to his boss that ridiculed his letter. "He didn't tell me about it first," Herhold says. "He was a nasty guy who played around your back."

Herhold edited Webb's stories for a year. The experience was "very painful," he says. "Gary needed a very strong editor, and I tried, but I don't think I was his match. I was still new as an editor. I don't think I knew enough to ask Gary to make the requisite phone calls to make his stories more fair."

A typical example, Herhold says, was Webb's story about then-Attorney General John VanDeKamp, who was engaged in a bitter race for governor. Through a public records act request, Webb obtained a list of cases VanDeKamp had declined to prosecute. "Gary did a big, long piece about all these cases and the nut of the piece was that VanDeKamp was a wimp," he says.

The story's timing helped Dianne Feinstein beat VanDeKamp in the 1990 Democratic primary. "If I were a stronger editor, I would have told Gary to talk to some other prosecutors," Herhold says. "That kind of innate sense of fairness didn't come naturally to Gary. He was a crusader."

In 1994, Webb wrote a series of articles about a failed effort by the California Department of Motor Vehicles (DMV) to revamp its aging network of mainframe computers. In the wake of "Dark Alliance," the *New York Times* would raise the series as yet another example of Webb's one-sidedness. The stories involved the fact that the DMV had spent millions of dollars on software that was supposed to solve the agency's legendarily inept record keeping. But the software had failed to noticeably improve the DMV's database. Webb had blamed the DMV fiasco on a corporation named Tandem Computers, Inc., which had written the software program; his reporting implied that Tandem had intentionally sold the DMV faulty software. After his stories were published, James Treybig, the company's founder, complained to Webb's editors about the story, and took out a two-page advertisement in the *Mercury News* refuting his coverage point by point.

A second reporter, Lee Gomes, investigated Treybig's complaint. Gomes came to the conclusion that Webb had gone into the story seeking to prove that Tandem was responsible, and had left out any information that showed otherwise. In fact, Gomes says, Tandem had done the best it could and the software had failed thanks to a complex array of unforeseen technical challenges. Gomes ultimately wrote a memo to his editors saying that one of Webb's stories was "in all its major elements, incorrect." A state audit later cleared the company of wrongdoing.

Now a San Francisco-based reporter for the *Wall Street Journal*, Gomes says that he wrote a lengthy story providing a full account of the DMV fiasco, but the *Mercury News* refused to publish it. Part of the reason for that, he says, is that his story was long and complicated. "But institutionally, the *Mercury News* wanted to circle the wagons," Gomes adds. "There wasn't an institutional interest in getting the opposing story."

Years later, when the *New York Times* interviewed Webb about Gomes and the Tandem controversy, Webb argued that Gomes was simply jealous because he had missed the story himself. "Whenever his reporting was challenged he always launched ad hominem attacks on people who challenged him, and he did that to me," Gomes says. "I thought he was a completely dishonest reporter. I didn't have a lot of respect for the guy and I think he's an example of everything a reporter shouldn't be."

"Gary was smart: he knew how to dig and how to use public records to get great stories," says Dawn Garcia, a former investigative reporter for the *San Francisco Chronicle*. Garcia became the *Mercury News'* state editor shortly after Herhold transferred out of the job in 1990. Now deputy director for Stanford University's John S. Knight Fellowships for Professional Journalists, Garcia says Webb, like a lot of investigative reporters, was passionate about his stories. "But he sometimes didn't see other points of view," she says. "I worked to help guard him against those instincts. That was one of my roles as his editor. I also learned pretty quickly that he had a temper and some editors did not like working with him."

At the time, Webb appeared to be languishing at the Sacramento bureau. Between the birth of his daughter, Christine, that year, and his difficult relationship with Herhold and other editors, Webb experienced his first bout of clinical depression. "It wasn't huge early on," Sue says. "He was just kind of moody, but after Christine was born, he started getting really depressed. It was a lot of pressure to have a baby, a two-and-a-half year old kid, and a six-year-old. We were both pretty overwhelmed."

To escape his depression, Webb buried himself in his work with renewed vigor, and under Garcia's tutelage, broke some impressive stories, including "The Forfeiture Racket," a 1994 expose of California's drug asset forfeiture laws, which allowed police to seize houses and other property belonging to suspected drug dealers. After the series ran, state lawmakers rescinded the forfeiture program, and Webb won the H.L. Mencken Award for reporting from the Free Press Association.

"Gary wasn't well known in the newsroom because he had never worked there," Garcia says. "As a bit of a loner, he did not have a big support network there." But after Gary won awards for his reporting on the state's drug forfeiture program, Garcia says, "his image was somewhat resurrected at the paper."

"The Forfeiture Racket" also bore a much more unexpected piece of fruit. One afternoon in July 1995, Webb arrived at his desk to find a pink slip bearing a telephone number from a woman named Coral Baca, whose boyfriend, a Nicaraguan drug dealer named Rafael Cornejo, had been one of the criminals targeted by the forfeiture program Webb had exposed. Baca wanted Webb to write about how the government had set up her boyfriend on bogus charges and then seized and sold his house.

Webb told Baca he didn't think his editors would be too interested in her story. He had already written as much about California's drug seizure laws as he was going to write. And an imprisoned drug dealer who says he's innocent? That didn't seem like news. But as Webb would later write in his 1998 book *Dark Alliance*, Baca quickly changed his mind. Webb was about to discover that this was the telephone call he had been waiting for his whole life, the one that his old friend at the *Plain Dealer*, Tom Andrzejewski, had jokingly anticipated every time he picked up the receiver.

"There's something about Rafael's case that I don't think you would have done before," Baca told Webb. "One of the government's witnesses is a guy who used to work with the CIA selling drugs. Tons of it . . . And now he's working for the government again."

Without realizing it, Webb had just stumbled onto "The Big One."

AT FIRST, CORAL Baca's tale of CIA-tied drug traffickers flooding the streets of San Francisco with cocaine seemed too strange to be true. She reminded Webb of a local conspiracy theorist who would bombard the *Mercury News* with wild allegations of secret government plots. Whenever the man demanded to speak with a reporter, he'd be unleashed on the newest hire—while everyone else in the office took bets on how long it would take for the unwitting subject of the bullshit detection test to realize the would-be source was nuts.

But Baca didn't seem crazy. She wasn't talking about theories, she was talking about a specific case—her boyfriend's—and claimed she had stacks of legal documents and Drug Enforcement Administration (DEA) records that would confirm that the chief witness against Rafael Cornejo sold drugs for the CIA.

After hanging up the phone, Webb did the first thing he always did when checking out a lead—he examined the public record for any information that would shed light on Baca's story. The first document he found was a recent *San Francisco Chronicle* article about a group of prisoners who tried to escape from a Bay Area federal prison. "Four inmates were indicted yesterday in connection with a bold plan to escape from the federal lockup in Pleasanton using plastic explosives and a helicopter that would have taken them to a cargo ship at sea," the *Chronicle* had reported. "Rafael Cornejo, 39, of Lafayette, an alleged cocaine kingpin with reputed ties to Nicaraguan drug traffickers and Panamanian money launderers, was among those indicted for conspiracy to escape."

Other stories described Cornejo as a member of a major West Coast drug ring that imported millions of dollars worth of cocaine from Cali, Colombia to California. Webb agreed to meet Baca and check out her documents. She gave him a stack of DEA and FBI reports that Cornejo's lawyers had obtained through discovery. One of them was a February 3, 1994 transcript from the federal grand jury probe of Cornejo's drug ring. It contained testimony from the government's chief witness against him, a Nicaraguan exile and drug trafficker named Oscar Danilo Blandon.

Then a twenty-seven-year-old son of a family of property owners, Blandon had fled Nicaragua just weeks after the 1979 Sandinista Revolution. His family was part of the land-owning aristocracy that had prospered under the dictatorship of the Somoza family. He had obtained a master's degree in marketing from a Colombian university in Bogota. Through his family's connections, he'd worked for the Somoza regime, providing U.S-supported food aid to the dictator's National Guard and administering a free-market rural development program aimed at increasing production among the commercial planters who had ruled the country with an iron grip for decades.

From the moment the Sandinistas seized power, civil war was inevitable in the tiny Central American country. The Sandinistas formed in the early 1960s as a tiny group of guerrillas inspired by the Cuban revolution, but their tenacious efforts to win power from a widely despised dictator gradually attracted broad-based support among Nicaraguans from all economic classes. After seizing power, however, many of the rebels' wealthy and middle-class supporters became disenchanted with the Sandinistas, their socially redistributive economic goals, and their professed admiration for Fidel Castro.

Blandon was just one of thousands of well-off Nicaraguans who fled the country for the United States, hoping to return someday to a "free" country, devoid of communist subversion. Like many exiles, Blandon also became active in supporting the Nicaraguan contras, a right-wing guerrilla army that aimed to restore "democracy" to Nicaragua. The contras had a powerful ally in the CIA, which was willing to work with just about any Nicaraguan, regardless of their ties to organized crime or human rights violations. While well known to reporters who covered the civil war in the field, the CIA's collusion with torturers and drug dealers among the contras had been hidden from the American public. Just about all the average American citizen knew about the contras was what President Ronald Reagan said about them in televised press conferences at the time: they were "freedom fighters" in the spirit of America's founding fathers.

In his testimony against Rafael Cornjeo, Blandon had stated under oath that he became a drug dealer shortly after arriving in the U.S. With the cash he raised, he purchased vehicles and other supplies for the contras. After it became clear that his support was no longer needed, he had continued dealing drugs, but kept the profits for himself. As Webb read through the thirty-nine-page grand jury transcript, it became clear that Cornejo wasn't actually the head of the drug trafficking ring the grand jury was probing. He noted repeated references to a certain Nicaraguan "family," but every time the prosecutor led Blandon in that direction, his responses were blacked out, deleted by government censors.

Webb later wrote that he asked Baca what family Blandon was talking about. "Rafael says it's Meneses—Norwin Meneses and his nephews," Baca said. "Norwin is one of the biggest traffickers on the West Coast. When Rafael got arrested, that's who the FBI and the IRS wanted to talk to him about." Intrigued, Webb showed up at the federal courthouse in San Francisco for one of Cornejo's hearings. But Blandon—the prosecution's main witness—was a no-show. During a break from the proceedings, Webb approached the prosecutor, U.S. attorney David Hall, and asked him about Blandon's whereabouts. According to Webb, Hall responded that he had no idea.

Not knowing what to think, Webb went back to his office

in Sacramento and called his boss, *Mercury News* state editor Dawn Garcia, and told him about Cornejo's case. Garcia, who had worked as an investigative reporter, recalled hearing about the CIA and the contras during the 1980s. She was interested. Webb told her that Blandon had been arrested in San Diego a few years ago, and asked for permission to go there and look for court records that might reveal more about him. Garcia approved the trip. "When Gary brought me his first tip about what was later to become 'Dark Alliance,' it sounded very intriguing," Garcia says. "I agreed he should go check it out."

Besides Garcia, the only person who knew the details of his project was Webb's wife. A licensed respiratory therapist, Sue never failed to be intrigued by his sordid accounts of official corruption. Throughout his career, every evening over dinner, she would ask her husband about his latest discoveries. But nothing could prepare her for what Webb told her about his story involving the CIA and drugs. "I thought it was the craziest thing I'd ever heard in my life," Sue recalls. "But after he got all these documents and started connecting the dots, I thought it was amazing."

A few days later, Webb flew to San Diego. At the federal courthouse there, he found records from Blandon's trial. Along with his wife, Blandon had been arrested with five other suspects for conspiring to distribute cocaine. Blandon looked like a big fish; according to the indictment, he was buying coke in wholesale quantities and selling it to other major traffickers. One of the records Webb found was a motion filed by Blandon's prosecutor, Assistant U.S. Attorney L. J. O'Neil, in opposition to Blandon's request to be released from prison on bail.

"Mr. Blandon's family was closely associated with the Somoza government that was overthrown in 1979," O'Neil claimed. "He is a large-scale cocaine trafficker and has been for some time." O'Neil's motion also stated that Blandon and another Nicaraguan, Jairo Meneses, a former commander in Somoza's National Guard, had been responsible for 764 kilos of cocaine seized in Nicaragua in 1991. The pair also owned hotels and casinos in Nicaragua that they had purchased after the Sandinistas were voted out of power in 1990. Meneses: Webb immediately recognized the name from his conversation with Baca about who really pulled the strings of her boyfriend Rafael Cornejo's cartel.

Blandon's lawyer, Bradley Brunon, didn't deny his client's ties to the Somoza regime. In his effort to win Blandon's release on bail, he introduced to the court record a photograph of Blandon at a wedding reception with Somoza and his wife. Brunon argued that Blandon's ties to Somoza proved that the allegations against him were "politically motivated because of Mr. Blandon's activities with the contras in the early 1980s."

The court file revealed that Blandon and his co-conspirators had never gone to trial. Instead, the suspects took plea deals that gave them relatively light sentences; Blandon had been ordered to serve 48 months behind bars, but the file showed that sentence was later cut in half—presumably because Blandon had become an informant. As Webb kept reading, he discovered that Blandon was already out of prison. By the government's own admission, he had been a major cocaine trafficker for roughly a decade, and had spent exactly twenty-eight months behind bars.

BACK IN SACRAMENTO, Webb began to investigate Norwin Meneses, whom Baca's boyfriend Cornejo had identified as the ringleader of his drug network. He quickly found newspaper articles from the *Chronicle* and *San Francisco Examiner* reporting that Meneses had been dealing cocaine for the contras throughout the 1980s. One story referred to Meneses as the "king of cocaine in Nicaragua" where he acted as the Cali cartel's Central American liaison for smuggling to the U.S. Another article mentioned that his name had come up in connection with a U.S. Senate investigation of contras and drug dealing in the late 1980s.

Webb hit the library and spent the next several days reading through roughly 1,100 pages of transcripts and exhibits from the U.S. Senate Subcommittee on Narcotics & Terrorism, better known as the Kerry Committee investigation. Led by Massachusetts Senator and future Democratic Presidential candidate John Kerry, the Senate Foreign Relations subcommittee had spent the better part of 1987 and 1988 digging into widespread allegations that the CIA-backed contras had engaged in drug trafficking on U.S. soil to support their cause.

Among other things, Kerry had uncovered evidence of Panamanian dictator Manuel Noriega's covert support for the contras and his ties to Colombian cocaine traffickers, much of which was used two years later to justify the U.S. invasion of Panama. The records were replete with testimony from contra leaders, drug traffickers and pilots, all of it under oath, regarding the covert smuggling of weapons on CIA cargo planes from the U.S. to Central America, with cocaine often coming back to military bases and remote airfields on the return flights.

Because of its sensitive nature, the committee, however, sealed most of the testimony and Kerry's investigation got scant play in the national news media. The Iran contra scandal had uncovered so much official wrongdoing already that Kerry found little political support even among Democrats for his efforts to force further disclosures about collusion with drug traffickers from the CIA or the Reagan White House.

Webb called Kerry's chief prosecutor, Jack Blum, a lawyer in Washington, D.C., and asked him if he had ever run across Norwin Meneses in his investigation. Blum remembered the name. In his 1998 book, *Dark Alliance*, Webb wrote that Blum told him that Ronald Reagan's Justice Department had stonewalled the Kerry investigation into Meneses, and he had eventually moved on to other targets. "There was a lot of weird stuff going on out on the West Coast," Blum said. "But after our experiences with Justice . . . we mainly concentrated on the cocaine coming into the East."

Webb remembered being glued to the television during the Iran contra hearings in 1987. According to Sue, he had taped them while at work and had watched them every night until the early hours of the morning. During a family vacation to North Carolina's Outer Banks with Tom Loftus, his friend and former colleague from the *Kentucky Post*, Webb had skipped the beach entirely, sitting inside a rented cottage, relishing the sight of Lieutenant Colonel Oliver North being grilled by lawmakers on national television. But Webb didn't remember seeing anything on television or reading anything in the newspapers about weapons and drugs being smuggled back and forth between the U.S. and Central America.

In a recent interview, Blum says Webb probably didn't see

much about the contra drug issue in the news, because nobody was really covering it. "We would have a day of hearings and the White House would call reporters and say 'This is insane stuff—don't listen to them,' and by and large the press bought it," he says. "The coverage stunk. It focused on how the witnesses weren't credible because they were drug dealers. I used to say to people who asked me why we had these 'flakes' as witnesses, 'Bring me a Lutheran pastor who was there when the drugs were unloaded in Miami and I'll call him as a witness.' These were the only witnesses we had."

One of the few reporters who had done their homework on the story was Robert Parry, an Associated Press reporter who had eventually quit his job when his own credibility was attacked by Reagan administration officials and their allies in the news media, particularly the right-wing *Washington Times*. Martha Honey, a *New York Times* stringer who lived in Costa Rica during the 1980s, had also done some reporting on the issue. She and her husband, Tony Avirgan, had been set up on phony drug charges after trying to prove the CIA was involved in drug trafficking.

Webb later wrote that he called Parry at his home in Alexandria, Virginia, and told him what he'd unearthed about Blandon and Meneses. "Why in the world would you want to go back into this?" Parry asked. Webb wanted to know if Parry had ever heard anything about the contras dealing drugs in the West Coast. "Not that I'm aware of," Parry said. "This is definitely a new angle. You think you can show it was being sold in L.A.?"

Now a freelance investigative reporter who runs his own

online magazine, *The Consortium*, Parry remembers getting a telephone call from Webb, and being impressed with his discoveries. "Brian Barger and I covered the external drug dealing activities of the contras," he says. "But we never knew what had happened internally, where the drugs ended up once they reached the United States."

Parry and Barger had done more than perhaps any other reporters to uncover drug smuggling by the Nicaraguan contras. In 1985, they wrote the first stories exposing the fact that a then-unknown Lieutenant in the Marine Corps named Oliver North was working for the Reagan Administration, covertly funneling weapons to the contras. That year, they also exposed a CIA memo, or "national intelligence estimate," showing the agency knew the contras were involved in drug dealing, but had done nothing to stop it.

The story almost didn't run. Parry's editor called him and said the article would have to be held unless he could find someone in the CIA to confirm the memo's accuracy. But meanwhile, the piece had been sent to the wire service's Latin American desk to be translated into Spanish. From there it was sent to newspapers throughout the Spanish-speaking world. Once his editors realized what had happened, they reluctantly allowed an English-language version to run.

For their efforts, Parry and Barger were subjected to personal attacks by the Reagan administration. Both reporters left AP; Parry ended up at *Newsweek*, where his editors weren't happy about his perceived obsession with the story. At one point, the magazine's top editor told Parry's boss that he had been at a dinner party with senior White House officials and had a "very unpleasant experience" because of Parry's work. While much of the pressure came from politicians, Parry says his fellow journalists did the dirty work. Both the *New York Times* and *Washington Post* essentially ignored his reporting, while the right-wing *Washington Times* openly ridiculed it.

"The most aggressive attacks came from the news media," Parry says. "It all started with the *Washington Times* claiming it had been disproved, but then the major news organizations piled on and acted like it was their job to put the story down." The strange thing, Parry says, was that after Webb's story appeared, the major newspapers pretended that they had already covered the story, and that the CIA had already admitted the contras were involved in drug trafficking. "But that's not how they reported the story at the time, when they were busy mocking Senator Kerry as a 'randy conspiracy buff,'" Parry says.

So when Webb called Parry nearly a decade later with an interest in advancing the CIA-contra story, Parry tried to warn him. "I asked him how his relationship was with his editors," Parry says. "He asked me what I meant. He seemed genuinely curious. I told him, 'You will be facing a serious counter-attack, because this has happened to everyone who had written about it.' And Gary said he had a good relationship with his editors. He was naïve. He had no idea what he was about to set off on, how his colleagues would go after him."

Martha Honey, now a research fellow with the Institute for Policy Studies, a liberal Washington, D.C., think tank, was also no stranger to the contra cocaine story. In May

1984, her husband, Tony Avirgan, a freelance cameraman, had been wounded at a press conference held in La Penca, Costa Rica by Eden Pastora, a former Sandinista guerrilla known as "Comandante Zero." Pastora had defected from the rebels after the Nicaraguan revolution and formed his own contra army. At the conference, he announced he would no longer accept aid from the CIA. Halfway through Pastora's speech, an explosion ripped through the crowd.

Pastora survived, but Honey began to investigate the attack for the *New York Times*, convinced it was the work of Comandante Zero's rivals in a separate CIA-backed contra faction. In the course of her investigation, Honey stumbled into a covert contra support operation at the sprawling ranch of John Hull, an American expatriate who lived on the Costa Rican border with Nicaragua. Honey's sources told her that Hull and a group of Cuban-Americans were using his ranch as a transshipment base to help the CIA supply the contras with weapons.

"We knew about the arms shipments, but started hearing about drug shipments too," Honey says. "It became clear that there was this whole network in Costa Rica on John Hull's farm. There were covert landing strips where this clandestine network was moving arms and men, but also drugs. Planes brought in supplies and left with drugs. It became clear that drugs were a central part of contra operations."

In 1985, Honey hired Daniel Sheehan, a crusading attorney with the Christic Institute, a public interest law firm founded five years earlier by Sheehan, his wife Sara Nelson, and William J. Davis, a Jesuit priest. The firm had already won public acclaim—and even inspired a Hollywood film—

for successfully suing the Kerr-McGee Nuclear Power Company on behalf of whistleblower Karen Silkwood. In the La Penca case, Sheehan began compiling the information Honey and Avirgan had unearthed about Hull and his cohorts, whom the couple was certain had been behind the bombing. The most intriguing evidence came from Jack Terrell, an employee of Rob Owen, who reported directly to Oliver North at the White House's National Security Council. Terrell, who later testified in congressional hearings, told Sheehan he witnessed Hull admitting responsibility for the bombing during a meeting in Costa Rica with a rival of Pastora, a contra leader and CIA asset named Adolfo Calero.

In Sheehan's mind, however, that testimony was just one small part of a much larger puzzle. Sheehan saw the La Penca incident as a perfect vehicle to expose a covert team he believed was operating on the fringes of the CIA and the White House, a crew that went all the way back to the Bay of Pigs, the agency's failed 1961 invasion of Cuba, and the covert war in Laos. In May 1986, Sheehan filed suit against Hull, Oliver North, and several Reagan administration officials later named as Iran contra conspirators, charging them with negligence in the bombing injuries suffered by Avirgan.

Shortly after Sheehan filed the lawsuit, Honey and Avirgan received a notice from the Costa Rican postal service that they had a package awaiting them at the custom's office. The couple sent their housekeeper to pick it up. Later that night, several customs police barged into their house and arrested them for drug possession. The package had contained a hollowed-out book full of cocaine and a purported note from a Sandinista leader. "Dear Tony and

Martha," it began. "Here is the latest sample of the shipment from Colombia we want you to test. If the quality is good enough, we will ship a ton to Miami, where it will be received by Senator Kerry."

The charges were later dropped when the Costa Rican authorities investigated the drug shipment and determined it was a set up aimed at discrediting a pair of law-abiding journalists. But meanwhile, one of the witnesses in Honey's lawsuit was killed, and several others received death threats and had to flee the country. Things didn't go much better in the courtroom. Judge James L. King granted Sheehan discovery power allowing him to examine government records about the bombing and, more importantly, to force high-ranking Reagan officials to submit to depositions.

Sheehan furiously began collecting additional affidavits, but somewhere in all the excitement, it became unclear what the lawsuit had to do with the La Penca bombing. After two years of increasingly wild-sounding allegations, King threw the case out of court. Sheehan appealed King's ruling, lost, and was ordered to pay the legal fees for the defendants: $1,034,381.35. Avirgan, Honey, and several other journalists later reinvestigated the La Penca bombing and came to the conclusion that the CIA most likely had nothing to do with it. Instead, they blamed the bombing on a newly discovered Argentinean who appeared to have ties to the Sandinistas.

Despite the fact that Honey now admits she was wrong in her belief that Hull or his friends in the Reagan administration had been behind the bombing—a fact that would tend to invalidate the entire lawsuit—she insists that the real reason Sheehan lost the case was because he had become

Blandon, he received a call from an attorney he knew in San Diego. The woman said Blandon was about to appear as a witness against her client, one of the Nicaraguans who had been busted with Blandon in San Diego a few years earlier.

The attorney added that Blandon was also being called to testify in the upcoming trial of one of the biggest crack dealers in the history of South Central Los Angeles, "Freeway" Ricky Ross. Webb knew the name from his investigation into California's drug forfeiture laws. Ross was an illiterate, but highly intelligent child of Texas sharecroppers, God-fearing farmers who lived in a boarded-up shack and raised Ross with the notion that the same fate awaited him.

Ross felt otherwise. After moving to Los Angeles, he became a tennis prodigy in high school but lost a college scholarship when his coach discovered he couldn't read. Faced with no lucrative employment prospects, Ross capitalized on his relationship with friends in the Crips street gang, the largest and most violent criminal organization in South Central Los Angeles, to establish himself as the area's most successful crack dealer. Ross was soft-spoken, but sophisticated and ruthless in his determination to rise above his sharecropper roots. As soon as he started dealing drugs, he began investing his profits in property along L.A.'s Harbor "Freeway," hence the nickname, "Freeway Rick."

By the time Ross' luck ran out in 1994, when he was arrested for distributing crack in Texas, Ross had become something of a local legend in Los Angeles. On December 20, the *LA Times* had published a 2,400-word profile of Ross that identified him the "king of crack" who was "key to the drug's spread" in that city. The story, written by *Times* staff writer Jesse Katz, appeared just after Ross' release from prison. Ross accompanied Katz to the tiny hamlet in rural Texas where he'd been born, shed a few tears, and told the reporter he planned to put his criminal past behind him and lend his entrepreneurial talents to legitimate business activity in Los Angeles.

According to Webb's lawyer friend, Blandon had been Ross' supplier during the 1980s. When Ross had been released from prison in March 1995, Blandon had pleaded for his help in unloading a major coke deal. Ross agreed to pick up $1 million worth of cocaine at a department store parking lot in San Diego. What Ross didn't know was that Blandon was now a paid DEA informant, helping the government arrange a "reverse sting," when a supplier sets up his underling.

Webb immediately called Alan Fenster, Ross' Beverly Hills-based attorney, and asked him what he knew about Blandon. At first, Fenster had no idea who Webb was talking about, but when Webb said he had heard that "Danilo" Blandon had been Ross' supplier, Fenster gasped with recognition. As is common in the paranoid culture of the illegal drug trade, Ross had only known Blandon by his first name.

A few hours later, Ross called Webb from inside the Metropolitan Detention Center in San Diego, where he was awaiting trial. In his book, Webb wrote that he pried Ross for information about his friend Danilo. "He was almost like a godfather to me," Ross said. "He's the one who got me going." Webb asked if it was true that Blandon was Ross' main cocaine source. "He was," Ross affirmed. "Everybody I knew, I knew through him. So really, he could be considered as my only source. In a sense, he was."

Webb flew down to San Diego to meet with Fenster and Ross, neither of whom had any idea that Blandon had testified about his involvement in raising money for the contras. "What would you say if I were to tell you that he was working for the contras, selling cocaine to help them buy weapons and supplies?" Webb asked. Ross giggled nervously. "I would say that was some fucked up shit there," he offered. "They say I sold dope all over, but man, I know he done sold ten times more than me."

In December 1995, Webb gathered his notes and documents and wrote a four-page memo to his editors, outlining his discoveries, an event he described three years later in his book, *Dark Alliance*. "This series will show that the dumping of cocaine on L.A.'s street gangs was the back end of a covert effort to arm and equip the CIA's raging army of anti-communist contra guerrillas," Webb wrote. "While there has long been solid—if largely ignored—evidence of a CIA-contra-cocaine connection, no one has ever asked the question: 'Where did all the cocaine go once it got here?' Now we know the answer."

Webb wanted the series to run in March 1996, when Ross was scheduled to face a federal jury on his latest charge of dealing crack—a so-called "third strike" offense that could send him to prison for the rest of his life. He asked for permission to fly down to Miami to interview some of Blandon's associates, and to travel to Nicaragua to interview Norwin Meneses, who was locked up inside a Managua jail.

"I believe it was at the request of managing editor David Yarnold, who was my boss, that Gary came into the newsroom and met with the two of us," says Dawn Garcia. "Yarnold read the memo, really liked the sound of the project, and said he wanted to be directly involved—that we should work through him. The project editor was not invited to the meeting." The uninvited project editor was Jonathan Krim, assistant editor for investigative projects, whose job was specifically to edit complex investigative series. According to several sources at the *Mercury News*, Yarnold and Krim didn't like each other—Krim felt Yarnold was unqualified, and Yarnold thought Krim was arrogant. Their mutual animosity would have disastrous consequences for "Dark Alliance."

As Webb later wrote in his book, Garcia and Yarnold were amazed with his discoveries. "Yarnold read the project memo, shook his head and grinned," Webb wrote. "'This is one hell of a story,' he said. 'How soon do you think you can complete it?' " Webb asked for some time to travel to Central America to do further reporting, and said he would start writing as soon as he got back. Yarnold approved the trip.

Webb arranged to work in Nicaragua with Georg Hodel, a Swiss journalist and friend of Martha Honey who had more than a decade of reporting experience in Central America. Webb's collaboration with Hodel, and the latter's involvement with the Christic Institute lawsuit as an investigator hired by Honey and Avirgan, would later be cited by Webb's critics as evidence that "Dark Alliance" was simply a recycling of a decade-old conspiracy theory. With Hodel's help, Webb flew to Managua hoping to interview Meneses, who had been arrested there four years earlier for smuggling 750 kilos of cocaine into the country.

Unlike Blandon, Meneses was more than happy to talk.

He proudly recalled his work on behalf of the contras. He said he agreed to help raise money for the rebels in 1982 or 1983, after meeting with Enrique Bermudez, Somoza's former military attaché, at a contra encampment in the Honduran jungle. At the time, Bermudez was a CIA asset, the agency's hand-picked leader of the *Fuerza Democratica Nicaraguense,* or FDN, the Nicaraguan Democratic Force, the largest and best-organized faction of the contras. His right hand man, Ricardo Lau, a former intelligence officer for Somoza's national guard, had ties to Salvadoran death squad founder Roberto D'Aubuisson, a former army major suspected in the 1980 slaying of Salvadoran archbishop Oscar Romero.

Webb had obtained a photograph showing Meneses with CIA asset and contra leader Adolfo Calero at a contra fundraising event in San Francisco. In Honduras, Meneses claimed, Bermudez appointed him chief of "intelligence and security" for the FDN in California. "Nobody [from California] would join the Contra forces down there without my knowledge and approval," he said. Meneses also reminisced about his homes in Northern California, and how he owned restaurants, bars, car lots, and factories throughout the Bay Area. "I even drove my own cars, registered in my name," he said.

Webb was amazed. He had DEA records showing that the U.S. government had implicated Meneses in forty-five separate investigations since 1974, but Meneses had been doing business there and living the high life—without a hitch. He had never spent a day in a U.S. prison or even been arrested. Webb later wrote that a Customs agent who had investigated Meneses in 1980 before being transferred to another city discovered that Meneses was still in business when he was reassigned to San Francisco years later. "I was sitting in some meetings and here's Meneses' name again," the agent told Webb. "And I can remember thinking, 'Holy cow, is this guy still around?'"

It seemed clear to Webb that Meneses had been enjoying a charmed life inside the U.S.—or maybe the lack of success in prosecuting him had more to do with Meneses' ties to the contras. During Meneses' 1992 trial in Nicaragua, though, his involvement with the anti-Sandinista rebels had come back to haunt him. Enrique Miranda, a former Nicaraguan military intelligence officer who had been Meneses' emissary to the cocaine cartel of Bogota, Colombia, had pleaded guilty to drug charges and agreed to cooperate against Meneses in exchange for a reduced sentence.

In a written statement to the jury, Miranda had accused Meneses of funding the contras with cocaine proceeds. "This operation, as Norwin told me, was executed with the collaboration of high-ranking Salvadoran military personnel," Miranda claimed. "They met with officials of the Salvadoran air force, who flew [planes] to Colombia and then left for the U.S., bound for an Air Force base in Texas, as he told me." Meneses refused to answer Miranda's allegations when Webb interviewed him. And when Webb and Hodel requested an interview with Miranda, they learned that Miranda had vanished while out on a weekend furlough. Stranger still, his jailers hadn't bothered reporting his absence until Webb showed up at the jail asking to see him.

*   *   *

SUCH SETBACKS DIDN'T dampen Webb's enthusiasm. Although he wanted his story to be published during Ross' trial in Los Angeles, he quickly realized that having Blandon on the witness stand would provide him with a unique opportunity as an investigative journalist. Blandon would not only have to answer questions, he would be under oath. So Webb provided Ross' defense attorney, Alan Fenster, a series of questions aimed at getting Blandon to reveal as much as possible about his ties to the CIA, his role in contra fundraising efforts, his relationship to Meneses, and the extent of his drug dealing during the 1980s. While unorthodox, Webb's opportunistic strategy was heartily endorsed by his editors. They saw it as exactly the kind of moxie required to get to the truth—perhaps the only way to force a recalcitrant conspirator like Blandon to fess up to his important role in the story.

Blandon arrived in the courtroom wearing a dark suit and aviator sunglasses. L. J. O'Neil, the deputy U.S. attorney prosecuting Ross—and who had previously sent Blandon to prison—did everything he could to block Fenster from grilling Blandon about his relationship to the CIA or Meneses, but the judge allowed many of the questions to go forward. On the witness stand, Blandon said he met Meneses through another contra activist, an old college classmate, who told him to pick Meneses up at the airport in Los Angeles.

"I picked him up, and he started telling me that we had to [raise] some money and send [it] to Honduras," Blandon testified. He acknowledged being at the meeting where

Meneses and Enrique Bermudez discussed contra
fundraising efforts. "There is a saying that the ends justify
the means," Blandon testified. "And that's what Mr.
Bermudez told us in Honduras, okay? So we started raising money for the contra revolution."

Upon arriving back in San Francisco, Blandon said,
Meneses taught him everything he knew about the cocaine
business and gave him two kilos of cocaine, the names of a
few customers in Los Angeles, and a one-way ticket south.
"Meneses was pushing me every week," he testified. "It
took me about three months, four months to sell those two
keys because I didn't know what to do. . . . In those days, two
keys was too heavy."

But Blandon was more of a skilled marketer than he
might have preferred to admit under oath. He quickly realized the easiest way to sell large quantities of cocaine was
to find someone else to sell it for him. In 1982 or 1983—
Blandon wasn't exactly sure—he found that person in "Freeway" Ricky Ross. Through middlemen, the two had already
been doing business, and after Blandon realized Ross' potential as a salesperson, they worked closely together for the
next several years. Things ran smoothly until October 27,
1986, when agents from the FBI, the IRS, local police, and
the Los Angeles County sheriff raided more than a dozen
locations connected to Blandon's drug operation. Thanks to
a Freedom of Information Act (FOIA) request Webb filed
with the National Archives for records from Special Prosecutor Lawrence Walsh's 1987 Iran contra report, he had
obtained a 1986 FBI report about the raid.

A search warrant affidavit from the raid showed that L.A.

County Sheriff's Department knew Blandon's activities were connected to the CIA-backed civil war in Nicaragua. "Danilo Blandon is in charge of a sophisticated cocaine smuggling and distribution organization operating in Southern California," it stated. "The monies gained from the sales of cocaine are transported to Florida and laundered through . . . a chain of banks in Florida . . . From this bank the monies are filtered to the Contra rebels to buy arms in the war in Nicaragua."

Blandon, his wife, and several of their Nicaraguan associates, were arrested on drug and weapons charges. Not arrested that day was Ronald Lister, a retired Laguna Beach police detective who ran a security company in Newport Beach and who had met Blandon through right-wing contra support circles in Los Angeles. As Blandon would testify in Ross' trial, Lister had supplied him with weapons and advanced security equipment such as police scanners, which Blandon then sold to Ross and other drug dealers.

But when deputies searched Lister's home, they didn't find any drugs. According to a police report from the raid, Lister claimed he knew his house was being watched and told deputies he worked for the CIA. Declaring that the agency wouldn't be happy about the cops harassing him, Lister even picked up the telephone and threatened to call his contact at the agency, a man named Scott Weekly. An FBI report Webb had obtained showed that Blandon's attorney, Bradley Brunon, had called the Sheriff's Department and claimed that the CIA had "winked" at Blandon's activities.

In a 1996 interview, Brunon told Webb that he met Lister shortly after Blandon was arrested in the 1986 raid.

Lister, Brunon said, "scared him," and he wasn't sure whether Lister was investigating Blandon or working with him. "It was just like the hair on the back of your neck goes up," Brunon said. "I never knew what his true role was. I mean he covertly insinuated that he was CIA. At least, if not a sworn agent, whatever the hell they do to get to become employees—some sort of operative."

Webb tracked down Lister's former boss, Neil Purcell, the former chief of the Laguna Beach police department, a cop who had achieved fame decades earlier for arresting Timothy Leary for pot possession. "The man in my opinion, is a lying, conniving, manipulative person who likes to play with people's minds," Purcell said of Lister. "He's very evasive and loves living on the edge. He's the biggest bullshitter that has ever been placed on this earth."

Purcell told Webb that Lister had left police work to provide security services to rich Iranians. Another former Laguna Beach police officer, Christopher Moore, claimed that Lister had hired him in 1982 and that he had traveled to El Salvador with Lister to meet with a potential client: Roberto D'Aubuisson, then the leader of the country's right-wing death squads. "That was probably the highlight of my life at that point," Moore told Webb. "There I was, a reserve officer who'd only been in the country for a couple of days, and I was sitting in this office in downtown San Salvador across the desk from the man who ran the death squads. He had a gun lying on the top of his desk and had these filing cabinets pushed up against the windows of the office so nobody could shoot through them."

To Webb, Lister's connection to Blandon was like the

proverbial "smoking gun," suggesting CIA involvement in the drug ring. He already had Blandon testifying that shortly after meeting with CIA asset Enrique Bermudez in Honduras, he had been schooled in drug trafficking by Norwin Meneses, the "king of cocaine" in Nicaragua. Webb knew that Blandon had for years supplied coke to Ross, the largest crack dealer in L.A. history. Now, Webb had evidence that with the help of his partner Lister, Blandon had even been selling weapons and anti-surveillance gear to South Central drug dealers.

The National Archives also gave Webb a 1987 FBI report containing interviews with Douglas Ainsworth, a San Francisco contra supporter who told agents that Meneses and Bermudez were dealing weapons and drugs. Webb located Ainsworth, and tried to get him to talk. "You're bringing up a very old nightmare here," Ainsworth told Webb in an interview cited in his book. "You have no idea what you're touching on here, Gary. No idea at all."

Webb asked Ainsworth what he meant. "I almost got killed," Ainsworth said. "I had friends in Central America who were killed. There was a Mexican reporter who was looking into one end of this, and he wound up dead." Webb insisted that if Blandon and Meneses were selling drugs in L.A., it was his job to uncover it. As Webb tells it, Ainsworth laughed. "Meneses was selling it all over the country!" he exclaimed. "It wasn't just L.A. It was national. And he was totally protected."

It all seemed like the twisted plot of a Hollywood movie or a sensational episode of *Miami Vice*. But to Webb, it was simple: he had just uncovered the final link in the CIA-contra-cocaine connection—where the drugs ended up once they reached U.S. soil—a crucial piece of the puzzle that had eluded every journalist and government prosecutor before him. "It was all out in the open now," Webb later wrote. "The [contras] had sold drugs to American citizens— mainly black Americans—and the CIA was on the hook for it: a CIA agent had given the goddamned order."

Webb thought back to all the "lies" that had been reported in the mainstream media suggesting that the CIA-drug connection was just a conspiracy theory. "All the bullshit that had been piled on the reporters, cops, and congressional investigators who'd tried to do an honest job and bring light into the dark swamp where covert operators and criminals colluded" had failed to stop him. "There was no denying it anymore," Webb concluded. "Now I was ready to write."

In a year of painstaking research, Webb had created history by uncovering the first direct evidence—documented by sworn testimony and law enforcement records—of Nicaraguan contra sympathizers selling cocaine on the streets of America to raise money for their CIA-backed cause. He had eyewitness testimony that Bermudez, a paid CIA asset, had advance knowledge of that activity, and he had uncovered compelling circumstantial evidence that the agency had not only failed to intervene, but had possibly even protected the drug ring's operations.

But in chasing after the story, Webb had taken a perilous turn towards risking his reputation on a story that rested heavily on the allegations of a trio of convicted felons. Webb aimed to expose the elusive, long sought after connection between the CIA, the contras, and cocaine, a dangerous

THE POWERFUL AND perennially award-winning *Los Angeles Times* had always overshadowed The *San Jose Mercury News*, California's second largest newspaper. Although it had several bureaus around the country and a reputation for solid investigative work, the paper had won only two Pulitzer prizes, one for Pete Carey's coverage of the 1986 downfall of Ferdinand Marcos in the Philippines, and one for the paper's team reporting on the 1989 Loma Prieta earthquake.

Silicon Valley in the mid-1990s was at the forefront of the digital revolution. Thanks to its proximity to the software headquarters of the world, the paper boasted unparalleled coverage of the computer industry and the most advanced Web site of any American newspaper. There was a feeling among reporters working there that the *Mercury News* was perfectly positioned to start competing directly with much larger newspapers. All it needed was one more Pulitzer to seal the deal.

"There was no question that the paper was very anxious to make a mark," says Bert Robinson, Webb's former colleague and now an assistant managing editor at the *Mercury News*. "People sort of felt that like the paper was really verging on moving into the upper tier." Webb, he adds, was specifically hired to make that happen. "Gary was supposed to find big stories," he says. "The paper was striving very hard to get better and attract more attention."

"It was an exciting time," says a former reporter who asked to remain anonymous. "This was definitely a newspaper on the make." Nobody defined the sense of journalistic ambition and craving for collegial respectability at the *Mercury News* than Jerry Ceppos, the paper's bespectacled executive editor, who would become a central player in the controversy over "Dark Alliance." A 1969 graduate of the University of Maryland, where he edited the college paper, Ceppos had risen quickly in journalism—perhaps too quickly. He held a series of editing jobs at the *Miami Herald* before joining the *Mercury News* in 1981 as an associate editor.

"Ceppos was a nice guy, but the joke was he just added commas to your stories," the former staffer says. "And he was a big wine guy. If you had a story about wine, he would make sure it ran on the front page." Ceppos has never spoken publicly about "Dark Alliance" since the scandal subsided and did not respond to interview requests.

Unlike Ceppos, Webb's boss, *Mercury News* state editor

Dawn Garcia, had extensive experience as an investigative reporter. She was also the paper's only female Latina editor, the former staffer says, which caused some resentment among the *Mercury News'* old guard of white male editors, who felt she was an "affirmative action hire." Among reporters, though Garcia was well liked, especially for her skills in marketing hard news stories to other editors and guaranteeing them front-page treatment.

Besides Garcia, the only other editor at the paper directly involved in editing "Dark Alliance" was managing editor David Yarnold, who had almost no reporting experience and only the thinnest of resumes as an editor. A staff photographer, Yarnold had been identified early in his career at the *Mercury News* as having potential as a manager. He had been promoted to head of the paper's graphics department before rotating through several editing positions in preparation for his rise to the top tiers of decision-making. Yarnold, who failed to respond to several interview requests, was widely considered to be a ruthless competitor obsessed with attaching his name to whatever project would win the paper its next Pulitzer Prize.

The timing of Webb's discovery about the CIA, the contras, and the crack-cocaine explosion, his instinctive passion for the story, the relative lack of reporting experience among top editors like Yarnold, and the competitive, secrecy-oriented atmosphere in the newsroom, would have fateful consequences for "Dark Alliance." Webb's editors had generously given him a year to report the story, and could now barely contain their excitement about publishing it. But the project remained under tight wraps.

"I was at an editors meeting where we were talking about projects," the former staffer who requested anonymity recalls. "I'll never forget that meeting." As editors outlined upcoming projects, Garcia hinted that Webb was working on a major exposé involving the CIA and drug trafficking in California. "I asked if this was going to win a Pulitzer," he says. "Dawn just smiled."

By then, Webb's former colleague at the Sacramento bureau, Bert Robinson, had become the *Mercury News*' government and politics editor after three years at the paper's Washington, D.C., bureau. "I remember knowing that he was working on the story, but I didn't know much about it," he says. "It was kind of a secretive process internally, which is very typical of investigations. Reporters are just as suspicious of their colleagues as the people they're writing about."

Jonathan Krim, the paper's assistant managing editor for projects, was supposed to be responsible for shepherding investigative stories. But because Yarnold wanted to handle the project himself and he didn't get along well with Krim, the latter editor played no role in editing Webb's story. Krim was regarded by writers as a tough and brilliant editor. But he lacked Yarnold's political skills and wasn't well liked by many reporters or fellow editors. "He and Yarnold were always at odds," the former staffer says. "Jonathan is a smart guy. If he was involved in 'Dark Alliance,' a lot of people thought all the problems that happened could have been avoided."

"The idea that Yarnold was in charge of this story—that's a scary thought," said another former reporter who asked not to be identified. The reporter recalled how Yarnold sparked a mini-revolt among reporters when he insisted that the paper run a light feature about a children's cartoon show in place of a more serious story. "I don't recall what news story it was that was bumped down below the fold," the reporter says. "But it got bumped in order to put a story on the front page about the Teenage Mutant Ninja Turtles. When that happened, a bunch of reporters at one of the news meetings started chanting, 'No More Turtles!' "

Krim, now head of the *Washington Post*'s online department, refused to discuss other editors including Yarnold, but confirmed he had no involvement in editing "Dark Alliance." "At that time, my brief was to run the investigative team and to consult with other desks on their investigative work if they desired," he says. "This project was held tightly under wraps. I knew of its existence, and knew vaguely the subject matter, but never saw any copy until it was published."

As Gary Webb sat down to write "Dark Alliance," he learned that "Freeway" Ricky Ross had been convicted of conspiring to sell cocaine—a third-strike offense that automatically carried a sentence of twenty-five years to life in prison. Alan Fenster's line of defense—that Danilo Blandon, the chief prosecution witness and his client's former supplier, had set up Ross—didn't sway the jury. Neither did Blandon's testimony about his ties to the CIA-backed Nicaraguan contras. The verdict didn't surprise Webb, but stirred him to write an exposé on Blandon that would reveal not only that Ross had been supplied by a Nicaraguan cocaine ring with ties to the CIA and the contras, but also say something damning about the U.S. war on drugs.

"I became convinced that the whole war on drugs, fifty years from now, we're going to look back on it like we look back on the McCarthy era, and say, 'How the fuck did we ever let this stuff get so out of hand?' " Webb told author Charles Bowden in 1998. "How come nobody stood up and said this is bullshit? I thought I had an obligation because I had the power at that point to tell people this is fucked up, to tell them 'Don't believe what you are being told about this war on drugs because it's a lie.' I didn't want to be one of those guys fifty years from now and people said, 'Why didn't you ever write anything?' "

In his first draft of "Dark Alliance," Webb laid out his story as a case study of the hypocrisy of the drug war, beginning it in the early 1980s with Blandon's involvement in the emergence of L.A.'s crack market and concluding it a decade later with Blandon's transformation from drug merchant to government informer and the passage of the anti-crack laws that were then packing the prisons with thousands of young black dealers. In April, Webb finished the drafts—roughly 12,000 words long—and sent them up to his editor, Dawn Garcia. "They were like nothing I had ever written before, and probably unlike anything my editors had ever grappled with either: a tale spanning more than a decade—the contra war and the crack explosion," he wrote. Those events, Webb acknowledged, were "seemingly unconnected social phenomena," but his story would prove they "were actually intertwined, thanks largely to government meddling."

Webb's original draft highlighted the CIA's involvement in the drug ring, but didn't assert that the agency had conspired with Blandon or Meneses, but rather that it knew about their activities. In his 1998 book, Webb wrote that he "never believed, and never wrote, that there was a grand CIA conspiracy behind the crack plague. Indeed the more I learned about the agency, the more certain of that I became. The CIA couldn't even mine a harbor without getting its trench coat stuck in its fly."

Rather than a CIA conspiracy to flood the streets of South Central Los Angeles with crack, Webb stated in his book *Dark Alliance* that what transpired was "a horrible accident of history" abetted by bad timing. "The contras just happened to pick the worst possible time ever to begin peddling cheap cocaine in black neighborhoods—unbridled criminal stupidity, cloaked in a blanket of national security," he wrote.

But it was clear from the beginning that Webb's editors were understandably more interested in the CIA's role in the story than the human interest angle focusing on Blandon's conversion from cocaine wholesaler to paid DEA informant, and his ultimate betrayal of Ross. When Garcia read the series, Webb recalled, she told him the story was too long. Webb had written the series in four parts, each installment running from between 2,400 to 3,200 words. "For a major metropolitan daily, that's not a lot of space," Webb wrote. "For the *Mercury*, though, it was as if I'd asked for the moon, a raise, a shower in my office, and an executive parking place all at the same time."

Garcia says her first reaction to Webb's draft was that it contained some amazing reporting. "Like most projects of its size, it needed a lot of editing," she says. "Plus, this series got complicated fast: it had dozens of players, referred to multiple documents and court cases and described events spanning decades and countries. It was the beginning of months of editing . . . I was trying hard to make the series not only bulletproof but understandable."

Besides editing "Dark Alliance," Garcia had other office pressures to contend with. She had been recently promoted from state editor to city editor, a much more demanding job that put her in charge of about forty reporters and editors and required her to handle several long-term story projects at once. Because the *Mercury News* hadn't filled her old position, Garcia had to juggle both jobs while also doing her best to edit "Dark Alliance." "To find time to edit drafts of Gary's project and do my new city editor job, I squeezed in time on either ends of my work day," Garcia says. "I came into work some days at 6 A.M. and stayed long after everyone had left. I thought if I just worked hard enough, everything was going to be fine."

When Garcia told Webb the story had to be cut substantially and run in three parts, Webb characteristically bristled at the notion. "I can't do it in less than four parts," he protested. Webb argued that cutting it would be a journalistic disaster. "The problem was that the believability of the story hinged on the weight of the evidence," he wrote. "Every fact that was cut would make the story appear more speculative than it really was."

With Garcia running interference for him with Yarnold, Webb haggled over the story's length for the next several weeks. Yarnold stuck to his guns: the story would have to run in three parts. So Webb combined the second and third parts into one long section and sent it back to Garcia—with predictable results. "This second part is kind of long," Webb claimed Garcia told him. "We need to cut it."

After more weeks of editorial jiu-jitsu, Webb announced that he could find nothing else to cut from the story without destroying it. Garcia finally relented, telling Webb he could repackage the story in four parts. But when he turned in a new draft, Garcia told him that Yarnold believed the story read too much like a feature—he wanted the first section to focus on the CIA and the contras and their ties to Blandon's drug ring. "The reason it's got a feature lead is because the series is a feature," Webb argued. "It's about the three men who started the L.A. crack market. That's the story I want to tell. If we turn this thing into a contra cocaine story, everyone is going to say, 'Oh that's old news.' "

But there was no dissuading Yarnold or Garcia. "Yarnold and I both agreed it should contain the strongest news that Gary's reporting would support," Garcia says. "Gary had written a narrative feature lead. When I told him it needed to be a harder-news lead, he flipped out. After some coaxing and cajoling, he finally agreed to write a hard-news lead. We would regret a couple of words in that lead for the rest of our lives."

Webb's lead sentence provocatively evoked what he had spelled out in his original project memo months earlier: the Blandon-Meneses-Ross drug ring represented the first documentation of the long-rumored connection between the CIA's war in Nicaragua and the crack epidemic in urban America. "For the better part of a decade," Webb wrote, "a Bay Area drug ring sold tons of cocaine to the Crips and Bloods street gangs of Los Angeles and funneled millions in drug profits to a Latin American guerrilla army run by the U.S. Central Intelligence Agency, a *Mercury News* investigation has found."

Although neither Webb nor his editors realized it at the time, that sentence was one of the most inflammatory introductions to a work of investigative reporting in the history of mainstream American daily journalism. Perhaps more than Webb's story itself, which was ultimately much more nuanced—some would say it failed to support its lead—this opening sentence would lead to an unprecedented explosion of public outrage and an unparalleled barrage of criticism from the nation's newspapers.

By late July, "Dark Alliance" had been edited and was scheduled to run on August 18. Webb knew that the story's controversial nature required an unconventional sales tactic. Working with a team of highly skilled technicians at the Mercury Center, the newspaper's online department, he arranged to have links on the *Mercury News* Web site to all the important documents cited in the story. The graphics team designed a logo for the story, as well as numerous maps showing how the Blandon-Meneses drug ring smuggled the cocaine from Colombia to the United States.

Scott Herhold, who had transferred out his job as state editor in 1990, spent the summer of 1996 overseeing the graphics department. He had no idea what Webb was doing at the time. "I remember Gary coming in and working with this artist," Herhold recalls. "They had this big graphic with arrows all over the place. I knew something big was coming down."

Meanwhile, however, Yarnold, the project's supervisor, had stopped paying any attention to the story. Garcia became suspicious when Yarnold stopped responding to her messages about "Dark Alliance." She had no clue what was going on until the paper announced that Yarnold had been promoted to a new corporate job with Knight Ridder's media arm. "I was all by myself," she says.

Just as Webb readied himself for a long-scheduled summer vacation, timed to take place a few weeks before the story's publication date, Garcia called with the news that Yarnold was out of the picture. But she assured Webb that his replacement, Paul Van Slambrouck, had read the story and was excited about it. Unlike Yarnold, Van Slambrouck had a long resume as a reporter, including years as a foreign correspondent in South Africa.

Van Slambrouck didn't respond to interview requests, but Garcia says he rescued "Dark Alliance." "He was taking on a new job, but generously spent a lot of time helping me corral this project into the paper," she says. Van Slambrouck wanted "Dark Alliance" to run in three installments, which meant the story would have to be cut by sixty-five column inches. He also wanted more discussion of the CIA's role in the drug ring higher up in the story. Again, Webb protested, sending an email to Garcia saying if there was that much fat that could be trimmed, "we both ought to quit right now because we obviously aren't doing our job right."

Meanwhile, Jerry Ceppos had only read parts of the story. And Jonathan Krim, the one person who many at the paper believed possessed the editing skills to inoculate the story against the criticism it later received was on vacation when it finally ran. "I was on vacation in Hawaii at the time, and read the excerpts that appeared in the Honolulu papers," Krim says. "Our procedures changed after 'Dark Alliance,' and then I vetted all project proposals and copy before [stories] ran, even if I was not directly involved in editing the material."

In the end, Webb relented. During his vacation at a beach house in North Carolina's Outer Banks, then in a motel room in Washington, D.C., and finally in the basement of Sue's parents' house in Indiana, he rewrote the series. "It was a mess," Sue recalls, adding that the family was also in the process of moving houses. "Dawn wanted him to stay and keep writing, but Gary told her no—he was going on vacation. The whole time we were on vacation, he was writing."

"It was horrible," Webb later recalled. "I had no way of telling what was being cut back at the *Mercury*, what was being put back in, or what was being rewritten." He was convinced his editors had no idea what they were doing. "Don't these people know what they're dealing with here?" he fumed. "Don't they realize the import of what we're printing?"

On August 17, the night before "Dark Alliance" appeared on newstands, Webb was at a party at the Indianapolis house of his high-school friend, Greg Wolf. At 2 AM, when it was midnight in San Jose, Webb went to a bedroom and plugged his laptop into the Internet, dialing up the *Mercury News'* Web site. Instead of the paper's normally more subdued Web site, the entire screen filled up with the headline "Dark Alliance: The Story Behind the Crack Explosion" and an iconic image of a man smoking a crack pipe superimposed on the CIA seal.

Webb was aware that his story would be controversial. From his conversations with Bob Parry and Martha Honey, he knew what had happened to other reporters who had written about the CIA's involvement with drugs. But as he scrolled down the computer screen, eagerly reading his story to see how it had finally turned out, he wasn't worried about the future.

The story looked solid after all—and it had the most impressive online graphics of any work of journalism ever published. There were links to his documents and sound files of Blandon testifying in court. "Dark Alliance" had finally been put to ink. Webb felt a huge rush of relief. He emailed his colleague, Goerg Hodel, still down in Nicaragua, to let him know the story was online. Then he turned off his computer, went back out to the party, and got drunk.

SEVEN

Crack in America

WHEN THE AUGUST 18, 1996, edition of the *San Jose Mercury News* arrived on doorsteps throughout Northern California, readers were greeted with the dark silhouette of a man smoking a crack pipe superimposed on the official seal of the CIA. In red and black lettering—the ominous, official style of type associated with top secret files—was the series' logo: "Dark Alliance: The Story Behind the Crack Explosion." Beneath were the words, "Day One: How a cocaine-for-weapons trade supported U.S. policy and undermined black America," and an even larger headline, "Crack Plague's Roots Are in Nicaraguan War." Readers were thus introduced to the most explosive journalistic exposé since the end of the Cold War.

As implied by the headlines and logo—neither of which

were created by Webb, but copy desk editors at the *Mercury News*—"Dark Alliance" promised to provide disturbing revelations about the CIA's involvement in America's crack-cocaine explosion. The first sentence left no doubt the story didn't just involve drug dealers, but the Langley, Virginia-based spook house: "For the better part of a decade, a San Francisco Bay Area drug ring sold tons of cocaine to the Crips and Bloods street gangs of Los Angeles and funneled millions in drug profits to a Latin American guerrilla army run by the U.S. Central Intelligence Agency, a *Mercury News* investigation has found."

The following two sentences were even more sweeping. "This drug network opened the first pipeline between Colombia's cocaine cartels and the black neighborhoods of Los Angeles, a city now known as the 'crack' capital of the world," the article stated. "The cocaine that flooded in helped spark a crack explosion in urban America . . . and provided the cash and connections needed for L.A.'s gangs to buy automatic weapons."

Along with the image combining the CIA seal with the crack addict and the lead sentence's claim that "millions in drug profits" from "tons of cocaine" had gone to the CIA-backed contras, those two sentences contained assertions that would later come to haunt Webb. The idea that Blandon and Meneses had together formed the first coke pipeline to urban America, thus sparking the crack "explosion" in inner cities across the country, was something that Webb and his editors surely believed, but which "Dark Alliance" neither explicitly stated nor proved.

What the story did prove was that two Nicaraguan contra

sympathizers had supplied "Freeway" Ricky Ross, L.A.'s most notorious crack dealer, with enough cheap cocaine to keep him in business for years, and that at least some of the profits helped the CIA fight communism in Central America. The first installment of the three-part series told how Blandon and Meneses had met at a contra base in Honduras with CIA asset Enrique Bermudez, whom Webb misidentified as a "CIA agent," before dealing coke to "Freeway" Ricky Ross—"a dope dealer of mythic proportions in the L.A. drug world" who "turned the cocaine powder into crack and wholesaled it to gangs across the country."

A sidebar to the story detailed how the drug ring had its own "little arsenal"—a steady supply of Uzis and other automatic weapons courtesy of Blandon's partner, Ronald Lister, the ex-Orange County cop who told Sheriff's Deputies raiding his home that he worked for the CIA. "We had our own little arsenal," Ross observed. "Once [Blandon] tried to sell [my partner] a grenade launcher. I said, 'Man, what [the fuck] do we need with a grenade launcher?'"

In late 1986, Webb reported, FBI agents investigating the Iran contra scandal interviewed Lister's former real estate agent, who said Lister paid cash for a $340,000 house in Mission Viejo. When the realtor asked Lister where the money came from, Lister had replied that he was involved in "CIA-approved" security work in Central America. Further evidence of Lister's "security" work came from Christopher Moore, who traveled to El Salvador in 1982 with Lister. Moore said that Lister was trying to provide security to a Salvadoran Air Force Base. "Lister always said he worked for the CIA," Moore stated. "I didn't know whether to believe him or not."

As if to explain why Lister would be pitching security work to a Salvadoran air base, Webb revealed that Blandon's partner Meneses was a friend of Marcos Aguado, a contra pilot who also worked for the Salvadoran Air Force. While flying weapons to the contras in Honduras, Aguado was stationed at the Ilopango Air Force Base. A covert area of the airport run by the Salvadoran military doubled as a major contra supply center. Ilopango was more than just a part of the contra weapons pipeline, however. According to Celerino Castillo, an ex-DEA agent then stationed in El Salvador, the base was also a locus of contra drug smuggling.

Castillo was a decorated Vietnam veteran and firm believer in the drug war. But when he tried to report his discoveries to his superiors, the DEA responded by opening an internal investigation of him, forcing him to resign his job. "Basically, the bottom line is it was a covert operation and they [DEA officials] were covering it up," Castillo told Webb. "You can't get any simpler than that. It was a cover-up."

The second installment of "Dark Alliance" told the story of Blandon's unlikely evolution from Ross' supplier to government informant and witness against "Freeway" Ricky Ross. The story also profiled Ross' equally unprobable rise from rural Texas to king of crack cocaine, and how his career ended shortly after his release from prison in Texas in 1994, when Blandon had asked for his help arranging a major drug deal. When Ross picked up the drugs, DEA agents arrested him. The final, and least controversial, installment of the of Webb's three-day series offered a dramatic critique of federal drug sentencing guidelines, and how stiffer penalties for crack as opposed to powder cocaine users and dealers had filled the nation's prisons with young inner city residents, the overwhelming majority of whom were African Americans.

At its best, "Dark Alliance" was a vivid, convincing account of how three drug dealers had wreaked havoc on America's inner cities and how their activities were closely tied to the CIA's war in Central America. But that narrative relied primarily on occasionally conflicting statements by convicted drug dealers. Webb supported their claims by citing law enforcement records suggesting that Blandon, Meneses, and Lister were involved with the CIA and were laundering millions of dollars of drug proceeds to support the agency's war in Nicaragua.

Yet nowhere in "Dark Alliance" was there any direct proof that the CIA had either participated in the drug trafficking Webb had uncovered or that the agency had even known about it. The lack of proof of CIA complicity and Webb's reliance on relatively few sources—combined with the story's sensational claim that three men inadvertently ignited the crack explosion—would provide ample ammunition for the "debunking" of "Dark Alliance" and the ultimate undoing of Gary Webb.

The initial reaction to "Dark Alliance" among Webb's colleagues was decidedly mixed. "When it came out, there was a sense of pride in the newspaper," says a former *Mercury News* reporter who requested anonymity. "It definitely caused a stir. My view was that, in a sense, it was an old story that had been ignored by the major newspapers. I had problems with some of the reporting, but thought it was basically right."

"Most people who read it initially thought it was very

good," says *Mercury News* assistant editor Bert Robinson. "But it was clear he had not tried very hard to get responses from the people he was criticizing. He hadn't really gone to the government—the CIA or anybody who was being shown up in this thing—to address the content of his reporting. Gary just thought that once you had the story, the people who were going to take the brunt of your reporting were just going to bullshit you, so it wasn't even worth bothering."

Mercury News investigative reporter Pete Carey recalls being impressed with the research Webb had compiled, which seemed to pull the curtain back from a decade-long cover-up of CIA-tied drug dealing. But he says he also noticed a major hole in the story. Too much of "Dark Alliance," Carey says, centered on what he considered unreliable testimony by convicted felons. Even the "federal law enforcement records" Webb referred to in his lead paragraph were mostly transcripts of testimony by crooks. "It concerned me because I saw the main sources on it were these two drug dealers," Carey says. "I wondered how far you could trust them. The fact that a drug dealer says something on a witness stand doesn't make it true."

In his 1998 book, Webb recalled how *Mercury News* executive editor Jerry Ceppos called to offer his personal congratulations. "Let's stay on top of this," Ceppos said. "Anything you need, let us know. We want to run with this thing." A few days later, Webb received a $50 bonus check and a note from Ceppos. "Remarkable series," it read. "Thanks for doing this for us."

Among the general public and Webb's fellow journalists, however, there was no immediate reaction. After a year of researching, writing, editing, and endless delays caused by his editors' desire to shorten the story's length and play up its newsworthiness, "Dark Alliance" had finally been published in the journalistic equivalent of a black hole, when most of America's national political establishment and the reporters who cover it are on vacation, fleeing Washington D.C.'s brutal late-August humidity.

The story also appeared in the week between the Democratic and Republican political conventions, so the few reporters who weren't at the beach were in Chicago covering the Democrats. The news that a regional newspaper in northern California had just published an article linking the CIA and the Nicaraguan contras to the street gangs of Los Angeles and America's crack epidemic had barely registered with the nation's political or media establishment. That didn't stop millions of people from reading it, however. "Dark Alliance" happened to be the first major investigative story published simultaneously in print and online.

"At first, nothing happened," Dawn Garcia, Webb's editor, recalls. "Then everything got pretty exciting and chaotic. Hundreds of phone calls started coming in to the newsroom from other media and from readers. It got so crazy I had to borrow somebody from the paper's marketing department to help answer all the calls from the media, supporters, and critics. It was starting to explode in a way that seemed good at the time."

THANKS TO THE Internet, still in its infancy at the time, "Dark Alliance" spread like wildfire. The Mercury Center, which previously had enjoyed just thousands of hits per day, suddenly was logging half a million daily readers from computers all over the world. Talk radio began picking up the story, and before long, the exposé was being highlighted in nightly news segments across the country. Although the nation's major newspapers were still ignoring "Dark Alliance," more and more people were reading it—a development that quickly made the series itself newsworthy. Some of the earliest commentary focused less on Webb's allegations than the fact that they had introduced many African Americans to the Internet.

The notion that the U.S. government had been somehow responsible for bringing crack cocaine to the inner city was nothing new—it had been a street rumor for years. In 1990, the *New York Times* surveyed more than 1,000 black residents of the Big Apple about their belief in "conspiracy theories." While only 10 percent of blacks said they believed the AIDS virus "was deliberately created in a laboratory to infect black people," a quarter of those surveyed believed the U.S. government "deliberately makes sure that drugs are easily available in poor black neighborhoods in order to harm black people." Only 4 percent of whites agreed.

"Dark Alliance" seemed to confirm what the African-American community had always felt about the U.S. government's complicity with drug smugglers and the racial hypocrisy of the war on drugs. The ferocity of the crack-cocaine problem in black neighborhoods meant there was hardly an African American in the country who didn't know someone either addicted to crack cocaine, selling it, in prison because of the drug, or dead from the gang warfare and criminal violence that accompanied its trade. Although the intensity of the response among black readers was unprecedented, both Webb and his editors must have suspected at least some of the anger it would unleash.

After all, the story's fall guy was Ross, the black street dealer, who had been supplied by wealthy Nicaraguans with powerful connections, and who had been ultimately taken down by the U.S. government and his former mentor Blandon, now a paid DEA informant. The outrage among the story's black readership may also have been bolstered by a link on the "Dark Alliance" Web site to a sound file of Blandon talking about how he liked like selling to "niggers" because they always paid in cash.

After the controversy began, Webb drew criticism for aligning himself with Los Angeles Congresswoman Maxine Waters and other black leaders who used his story to claim the CIA was directly responsible for addicting countless African Americans to crack. Although Webb didn't share all their suspicions, he saw their interest in the story as a tool that would help force the CIA to admit that they had turned a blind eye to Nicaraguan contra drug dealers, including Meneses and Blandon.

Webb had no ally more powerful or motivated than Waters herself. "They came in with the drugs," Waters said at one 1996 press conference. "They came in with the guns. They made the money. And boy, what did they leave in the wake? A trail of devastation, addictions, killings, crack babies. It's awful. It's unconscionable. And I'm committed—if I have to spend the rest of my life getting to the bottom of it, I intend to do that."

Maxine Waters did not respond to interview requests. Many of Webb's friends and family members weren't too happy about what they viewed as political opportunism by her and other public figures. "Gary didn't say the CIA was selling drugs, which is what everyone seemed to think," says Webb's high school friend Greg Wolf. "He said they might have turned a blind eye to it. People were trying to quote him to prove whatever point they wanted, that white people were trying to exterminate black people." Anita Webb felt that this ultimately helped the media discredit her son. "I don't think it's good that people grabbed on to this story and made it a black issue," she says. "The black community said the CIA was trying to do away with blacks, and Gary never said that."

Tom Suddes, Webb's former colleague at the *Cleveland Plain Dealer*, who had covered urban unrest for the paper, takes a more sympathetic view of the way African Americans reacted to "Dark Alliance." "The level of despair in the black neighborhoods was so incredible," he says. "They thought nobody was ever going to listen to them about the destruction of their own communities. To have a big mainstream paper talking about this—black males being assassinated by each other, a whole people going through this holocaust? Thank god, finally someone is paying attention. It wasn't paranoia or conspiracy theories—it was the destruction of a whole generation of people."

In Los Angeles, angry residents and members of the left-wing Crack the CIA Coalition held candlelight vigils and staged marches to city hall. L.A.'s city council passed a resolution demanding a federal investigation, and both California Senators Dianne Feinstein and Barbara Boxer called for Congressional hearings. On Capitol Hill, Waters held a press conference promising she would lead that effort. Cynthia McKinney, the outspoken U.S. representative from Georgia, publicly exclaimed on the floor of Congress that the initials CIA actually stood for "Central Intoxication Agency." Others quipped that the pseudonym stood for "Crack in America." Webb liked the riff. In an online forum to his story posted on the *Mercury News* Web site, he appropriated the line—a sarcastic miscue that wouldn't go unnoticed by the *LA Times*, which later used it to suggest Webb had gone off the deep end.

The hearings, conducted by the U.S. Senate Select Committee on Intelligence, took place in October and November 1996. They produced mostly predictable results. CIA Inspector General Frederick Hitz swore his agency would conduct an internal review that would unflinchingly answer Webb's allegations. Referring to the photograph of himself and Meneses at a party in San Francisco that had decorated "Dark Alliance," Contra leader Adolfo Calero testified that he attended countless fundraising parties in the 1980s and couldn't be expected to know everyone's background. Pastora—the famed "Comandante Zero"—was more forthcoming. He acknowledged receiving a few trucks and tens of thousands of dollars from Blandon, and added that Blandon had even allowed him the use of his villa in Costa Rica. Yet both leaders downplayed Meneses and Blandon's standing as contra fundraisers and strongly denied ever knowingly working with drug dealers.

Jack Blum, the former Kerry Committee prosecutor, was in some ways the star witness of the hearing. He testified that his investigation had never uncovered any direct CIA involvement with drug traffickers. "If you ask the question, did the CIA sell drugs in the black neighborhoods of Los

Angeles to finance the contra war, then the answer is a catagorical no," he testified. But Blum quickly added that the agency had known about contra drug trafficking and had done nothing to stop it. "When people who are engaged in an operation say, 'We're going to look the other way—we're not going to do anything,' interfere in the law enforcement process to protect people who are running the operation, and in that process of interference permit drugs to flow in, you have an extraordinary problem," he said.

Blum now says the hearing was more intense than anything he experienced during his fourteen-year career working in the U.S. Senate. "We had a roomful of angry African Americans hanging on my every word," he says, adding that most of the audience wasn't happy that he didn't defend "Dark Alliance." The story, Blum believes, missed the mark. There had been a cover-up of CIA ties to drug traffickers during the 1980s, but Webb hadn't proved this activity enabled the crack-cocaine epidemic.

But the reaction by the committee to his allegation that the CIA had turned a blind eye to contra drug smuggling struck Blum as at best naïve and at worst, a complete charade. "I was telling a story that nobody in the room wanted to hear," he says. "The committee was acting stunned about my remarks. It showed the pathetic nature of oversight of the Senate intelligence committee. Everybody runs around shocked that this stuff is happening, but it's been happening for years."

As the anger built in black communities, particularly in South Central Los Angeles, CIA Director John Deutch flew to Los Angeles to appear at a town hall meeting in an auditorium at South Central L.A.'s Locke High School—the first time in

American history that a journalist had forced the director of the world's most powerful spy agency to perform in-person, street-level damage control. More than five hundred people packed the audience. The booing began even before Deutch promised the crowd he'd "get to the bottom" of Webb's allegations, and grew even louder when he asserted his certainty that the CIA had no connection with the city's crack trade.

In a sworn declaration responding to "Dark Alliance," the CIA already had announced that it had reviewed its files and found no evidence the CIA had any ties to Ross, Blandon, Meneses, Lister, or the latter's supposed CIA contact, Scott Weekly. Perhaps forgetting that the agency had already acknowledged occasionally working with known drug traffickers in Vietnam, Laos, Afghanistan, and Central America, Deutch went even further. "As of today, we have no evidence of a conspiracy led by the CIA to engage and encourage drug trafficking in Nicaragua or elsewhere in Latin America, during this or any other period," he declared.

Deutch's demonstrably false assertion only further enraged his audience. According to Jim Crogan and Kevin Uhrich of *LA Weekly*, the CIA director's foray to South Central "went about as well as the agency's adventures in Vietnam, or Latin America, or Iran." One man interrupted Deutch, calling his appearance "nothing but a public-relations" stunt. "After all that illegal stuff we know you CIA people have done around the world, you tell us now that you're honestly going to investigate yourselves about drug dealing?" he shouted. "You gotta be crazy if you think we're going to believe that."

Also in the crowd was Michael Ruppert, a bespectacled,

sincere-seeming, middle-aged white man. Halfway through Deutch's speech, Ruppert stood up and accused the CIA director of lying. A former narcotics officer with the Los Angeles police, Ruppert later claimed he knew the agency was involved in the coke trade, and could prove it. Deustch listened politely as Ruppert detailed various cases he had unearthed as a police detective where the agency had colluded with drug dealers. Ruppert had left the department for personal reasons after accusing his department of colluding with drug traffickers, including his estranged girlfriend, whom Ruppert believed was a CIA agent.

Ruppert saw "Dark Alliance" as personal and professional vindication. In the aftermath of the controversy, he attached himself to Webb's story. Ruppert also insinuated himself into a grassroots effort to establish a Citizen's Truth Commission on CIA involvement in drug dealing. The inquiry ultimately fell apart because of a power struggle between left-wing revolutionary groups like the Crack the CIA Coalition and liberal organizations like the Institute for Policy Studies (IPS).

"I didn't think the commission was a particularly good idea," says Sanho Tree, an IPS drug policy expert who had been brought to the project by former freelance journalist Martha Honey. "The issue had already gotten out of control thanks to the nutters on the extremes. The story had become radioactive," says Tree. "I would talk to activists in South Central who were thoroughly indoctrinated by Ruppert. They told me that not a rock of crack cocaine was sold in L.A. without the CIA's permission. I told them people in Langley didn't know where South Central was, and they were trying to fund an illegal war, not trying to start the crack-cocaine epidemic."

Besides Ruppert, countless people of all political stripes came forward in the wake of "Dark Alliance" to use Webb's story to bolster their long-held suspicion that the CIA was secretly pulling the strings of world events. "Dark Alliance" had the uncanny effect of uniting conspiracy theorists on both ends of the political spectrum. In a way never seen before or since, it created an alliance of wild-eyed, would-be revolutionaries on the left who believed the CIA had deliberately started the crack epidemic to commit genocide against black people, and right-wing followers of Lyndon LaRouche, who saw the story as further proof that George Bush, Sr. and the Queen of England belong to a secret cabal that controls the planet.

"Ruppert and the LaRouchians were responsible more than anyone for Webb's downfall," says Tree, adding that the Citizen Truth Commission ultimately focused less on arguing over how much further Webb should have gone with "Dark Alliance" than in examining the inequities of the war on drugs. Meanwhile, Ruppert used the story as a launching pad for his online newsletter, *From the Wilderness*, which he has used to publicize various conspiracy theories.

Reached by telephone at the *From the Wilderness* office in Ashland, Oregon, Ruppert claimed someone had just smashed every computer terminal in his office. "It was an organized job," he said. He speculated that the vandalism either involved his efforts to expose government wrongdoing or a disgruntled former employee with ties to a local drug ring. He recently published a book about 9/11, *Crossing the Rubicon*, copies of which he brought to Webb's funeral. He credits "Dark Alliance" with not only jump-starting his publishing career but saving his life.

"I was going to commit suicide the week those stories broke," he says. "I had been trying for eighteen years at that point to expose CIA drug trafficking. I was living in this ramshackle place in Sylmar when I turned on the radio and heard about this major story in the *San Jose Mercury News* tying the CIA to cocaine shipments, and I ran out to get the paper. It kept me going. Somebody else had shown up and done the same work, and now there was credible evidence."

Ruppert chafes at those who call him a conspiracy theorist. "I come from a CIA family," he says. "The CIA tried to recruit me twice, when I was at UCLA and again through [my girlfriend] when I was at the LAPD." He claims IPS betrayed the groundswell of public demands for justice that arose in the wake of Webb's reporting. "They ignored me completely," he says. "I considered IPS to be a gatekeeping organization that was there to do damage control, and that's exactly what they did."

While Ruppert's sincerity as a whistleblower is something only he can address, his outburst at Locke High School and later, his self-promoting defense of Webb, didn't exactly help build credibility for "Dark Alliance."

FEW PEOPLE WERE more passionate about "Dark Alliance" than Joe Madison, "The Black Eagle," a radio talk-show host based in Washington, D.C., who now broadcasts on XM satellite radio. In a recent interview, Madison acknowledged that many African Americans, including some of his friends, took Webb's story further than the facts allowed, and that Webb had often chastised him when he inadvertently mischaracterized elements of the story. He says he became obsessed with "Dark Alliance" because it was the first time a mainstream American newspaper had taken a serious look at U.S. government complicity in the crack plague.

"In the black community, we always had suspicions," Madison says. "The old adage was that we don't grow cocaine. How could so much of it get into the country without the government knowing about it? It appeared that the black community had been targeted, and that this story was a major breakthrough."

Madison wasn't just a talk show host. A veteran civil rights organizer, he saw the controversy over "Dark Alliance" as an opportunity to rally America's black leadership in a quest for social justice. He called every black leader he knew—Maxine Waters, Jesse Jackson, Julian Bond, and Dick Gregory, a comedian turned social activist who in 1968 had run unsuccessfully for president as a write-in candidate for the Freedom and Peace Party.

When Madison reached him, Gregory was at the Democratic Convention in Chicago. He agreed to fly back to D.C. to join Madison in what turned out to be a two-man protest at CIA headquarters. "Dick and I went to CIA headquarters and began picketing," Madison recalls. "We pulled out a roll of yellow police tape that said 'This is a Crime Scene.' We had a copy of 'Dark Alliance' and demanded to see the director of the CIA to have him explain things. Needless to say we didn't get a meeting with him."

When Madison and Gregory tried to stretch the police tape across the gate at the entrance to the CIA, federal marshals arrested them for trespassing. "Most people thought we were out of our minds because you don't mess with the CIA," he says. Madison was released after two days, but Gregory continued to be held at a federal holding cell in Alexandria, Virginia. Madison showed up at a meeting of the Congressional Black Caucus, where he announced that Gregory was still behind bars.

"All hell broke loose," he says. "The next day, they released Dick, and we really began our campaign." Madison talked about the story every day for the next six months on his radio show, interviewing Webb and any guest who he could find who claimed to know something about CIA complicity in drug trafficking. As it happened, Oliver North hosted his own show at the same radio station where Madison worked at the time. When North agreed to debate Madison on C-SPAN, Madison used his time to read passages from North's Iran contra-era diaries that discussed his knowledge, lack of concern and possible complicity in covering up drug dealing by Panamanian dictator Manuel Noriega and various contra supporters.

Back in Los Angeles, Congresswoman Waters and several members of her staff arrived unannounced at the L.A. County Sheriff's Department. She demanded access to the agency's files from its October 1986 raids against Blandon and his henchmen. At first, a records officer insisted that no such raids had taken place, but Waters refused to leave empty handed. After receiving a box full of police reports, evidence lists and search warrant affidavits, Waters held an October 7 press conference announcing that she had uncovered further evidence of CIA complicity in the drug ring.

Waters was referring to the Sheriff Department's file she

obtained on its search of Ronald Lister's home. A few weeks before Waters held her press conference, Webb had published a follow-up story about Lister. Several of the sheriff's deputies involved in the raids were later arrested and charged with corruption for stealing money from drug dealers. During their 1990 trial, defense attorney Harlan Braun wrote a memo referring to Lister, and said his clients had evidence the CIA was involved in drug trafficking. Braun added that the evidence seized by the deputies mysteriously disappeared from an evidence locker within forty-eight hours.

Among the documents, Braun had claimed, were lists of CIA operatives in Iran, detailed inventories of weapons, ammunition, military hardware, and sophisticated surveillance gear, a diagram of money laundering routes, films of military operations in Central America, and technical manuals. Officers also discovered blown-up pictures of Lister posing with contra rebels at a jungle camp. To Waters, Lister's claim that he worked for the CIA—and the evidence apparently seized at his house in 1986—was nothing short of a smoking gun proving CIA involvement in L.A.'s crack epidemic.

In just a few months, "Dark Alliance" had evolved from a front-page story in a regional newspaper to a racially charged national controversy. Webb fielded interview requests from *60 Minutes*, *Dateline*, Jerry Springer, Geraldo Rivera, Tom Snyder, and Jesse Jackson. Montel Williams did a two-day special and personally interviewed Ricky Ross inside the Metropolitan Detention Center in San Diego. Whenever his hosts asked Webb what role the CIA had in selling drugs, he gave the same response: that was the one thing he hadn't been able to determine.

Not all the coverage was positive. Chris Matthews, the blowhard host of MSNBC's *Hardball*, blasted away at Webb for suggesting the contras resorted to selling drugs when they were flush with money from the Reagan administration. But when both Webb and another guest, Jack White of *Time* magazine, pointed out that the Boland Amendment, passed by the U.S. Congress in 1984, had prohibited the CIA from funding the contras, Matthews, uncharacteristically, was at a loss for words. During a break, he angrily berated his staff during a commercial break for "sabotaging" his show.

Yet the nation's major newspapers—the *Washington Post*, *New York Times*, and *Los Angeles Times*—still hadn't printed a word about Webb's story. The exception was a brief account in the *LA Times* about a protest in downtown Los Angeles. Conservative pundits like Bernard Kalb were dumbfounded. "Where's the rebuttal?" he asked a panel of reporters on CNN's *Reliable Sources*. "Why hasn't the media rose in revolt against this story?"

Kalb needn't have worried. The big papers were aware they had to come up with a response to "Dark Alliance." They had assigned their most experienced reporters—veteran journalists including correspondents with close contacts at the CIA—and tasked them with investigating Webb's allegations. When the big papers did weigh in, their combined response would represent one of the most withering deconstructions of an investigative news story—and perhaps the most unrelenting attack against a reporter's credibility—in the recent annals of American journalism.

Last family photo of Gary, November 10, 2004.
Gary, brother Kurt, Sue, mother Anita,
nephew Phoenix, son Ian, son Eric,
niece Renee, and daughter Christine

Gary with daughter Christine, 2003

Gary, 8 years old

Kurt and Gary (holding dog), 6 years old

Gary with mother Anita, father Bill,
and Kurt, Thanksgiving 1970

Gary with kids, 2000

Gary and Sue in Mexico, summer 2001

Gary, Cleveland Plain Dealer, mid-80s

Family photo: Anita with Eric, Sue, Gary, Kurt with Ian, 1990

Gary, *Kentucky Post*, 1980

Gary, *Kentucky Post*, Feb 1983

Wedding picture, February 10, 1979, maid of honor
Kellie Kilrain, best man Greg Wolf

Gary, Sue, Ian, Eric, and Christine at
Kurt and Diana's wedding, 1995

Gary, *Kentucky Post*, 1980

EIGHT

Feeding Frenzy

IT WAS ALREADY mid-afternoon when Jerry Ceppos arrived at the headquarters of the *San Jose Mercury News* on Sunday, October 3, 1996. As he did every day, Ceppos examined the incoming wire reports to see what stories the nation's big newspapers would break the following morning. A few minutes later, Ceppos calmly strode out of his office, clutching an advance copy of the *Washington Post*'s front-page run list.

"Jerry came over to me and told me they were going to do a knockdown on Webb's story," says a former *Mercury News* staffer who was sitting at his desk nearby. " 'What are you going to do about it,' I asked, and he said, 'If you have any great ideas, let me know.' "

At that moment, Webb was sitting inside an NBC green

room at Rockefeller Center in Manhattan, preparing for a guest appearance on *The Montel Williams Show*. Ceppos called Webb at the studio, and told him that the *Post* was going to run a story the next morning that was highly critical of "Dark Alliance." Webb asked what errors the *Post* had uncovered in his story. "They don't say the facts are wrong," Webb later quoted Ceppos. "They just don't agree with our conclusions." When Webb asked what evidence the *Post* had cited in reaching that particular conclusion, Ceppos responded, "A lot of unnamed sources, mainly. It's really a strange piece."

Dawn Garcia says the *Post* article took her completely by surprise. "What I had hoped would happen after 'Dark Alliance' was published is that other media would pick this up and run with it and continue the work we had started," she says. Both she and Webb thought that, once they jumped on the story, the nation's big newspapers, which had far greater resources to pursue the story, would inevitably advance it. "We had no inkling that *we* would become the story," she says.

Written by Walter Pincus and Roberto Suro, with the help of Douglas Farah, a correspondent in Nicaragua, the story, "The CIA and Crack: Evidence is Lacking of Alleged Plot," cited numerous and mostly unnamed sources who claimed that Webb was wrong. "A *Washington Post* investigation into Ross, Blandon, Meneses, and the U.S. cocaine market in the 1980s found that the available information does not support the conclusion that the CIA-backed contras— or Nicaraguans in general—played a major role in the emergence of crack as a narcotic in widespread use across the United States," the *Post* reported.

According to Pincus and Suro, while Nicaraguans "took part" in drug trafficking during the 1980s, "most of the cocaine trade" involved Colombian and Mexican smugglers, and domestic dealers whose ranks included Jamaicans, Dominicans, Haitians, and "Americans of varying backgrounds." The statement ignored the fact that while "Dark Alliance" had mostly focused on two Nicaraguans—Blandon and Meneses—the pair's drug ring included Colombian suppliers, Nicaraguan middlemen, and African-American crack dealers—even a white ex-Orange County cop.

Citing unnamed "law enforcement officials," Pincus and Suro claimed that Blandon had sent only $30,000 to $60,000 in drug profits to the contras, and had only moved five tons of cocaine during his decade-long career. At one point in his testimony, Blandon had stated that he stopped funding the contras when President Reagan had been elected. If so, that would mean Blandon had started keeping his drug profits either before he and Meneses met CIA asset Enrique Bermudez in 1982 or 1983—or only about a year after that meeting, when Reagan won re-election. Either way, the *Post* concluded, Blandon hadn't been sending coke money to the contras as long as Webb had alleged in "Dark Alliance."

But just as Webb had highlighted the portions of Blandon's testimony that tended to show his illicit contra fundraising had lasted the "better part of a decade," the *Post* article focused exclusively on statements Blandon made that tended to minimize how much cash actually went to the rebels. In using Blandon's testimony to undermine Webb's story, Pincus and Suro also did exactly what Webb got in

trouble for doing—basing broad conclusions on the testimony of a drug dealer. And in quoting anonymous law
enforcement officials about the amount of cash that funded
the rebels, the *Post* neglected to account for the 1986 L.A.
County Sheriff's Department records cited by Webb, which
clearly stated that Blandon was still dealing large amounts
of cocaine that year and still sending the profits to the contras through a chain of banks in Florida.

Pincus and Suro also questioned Webb's ethics, citing his
intervention in Ross' criminal trial. They interviewed Ceppos,
and quoted him saying that while he "did not know" Webb had
fed questions to Alan Fenster, Ross' attorney, he didn't see any
ethical problems with such tactics. At first Ceppos was glad the
Post was jumping on the story, but such questions provided
the first inkling that the coverage wasn't going to be positive. It's
possible Pincus and Suro got their tip on Webb's courtroom
behavior from Post media critic Howard Kurtz, who a few
days earlier, wrote the paper's first story questioning Webb's perceived one-sidedness by noting that, "[fr]rom the beginning,
Webb appeared conscious of making news." Specifically,
Kurtz reported, Webb had written Ross a letter asserting that,
"in terms of generating public interest," it was best to publish
the series "as near as possible to a newsworthy event—in this
case, your sentencing." By being the first reporter to question
not just "Dark Alliance" but Webb's professional conduct and
objectivity, Kurtz set the abrasive tone for future criticism.

"My initial impression of [Webb] was of a passionate journalist who worked hard and deeply believed in what he was
doing," Kurtz said in a recent interview. " 'Dark Alliance'
clearly tapped into some strong sentiments in the black community, elements of which wanted to believe what Webb was

implying but could not prove. I think Webb did overreach with the series, even as he insisted he wasn't explicitly saying what the conspiracy theorists believed he was. But the *Mercury News* editors were also responsible in the way they packaged the series and for not asking tougher questions and engaging in more rigorous editing. The newspaper would later acknowledge its failure, but Webb never really did."

At first, Webb's editors staunchly defended their star reporter. A few days after the *Post* article appeared, Ceppos sent an angry letter to the editor of the *Post* taking issue with the story's headline claiming "Dark Alliance" had alleged that the CIA had engaged in a "plot" with the drug dealers mentioned in the story. "While there is considerable circumstantial evidence of CIA involvement with the leaders of this drug ring, we never reached or reported any definitive conclusion on CIA involvement," he argued. "We reported that men selling cocaine in Los Angeles met with people on the CIA payroll. We reported that the money raised was sent to a CIA-run operation. But we did not go further."

Ceppos also tacked his letter to the *Post* to a bulletin board in the *Mercury News*, and attached another memo addressed to his staff that defended the series. "I'm not sure how many of us could sustain such a microscopic examination of our work and I believe Gary Webb deserves recognition for surviving unscathed," Ceppos wrote. But the *Post* refused to run Ceppos letter. "I couldn't believe it," Garcia says. "After running multiple critiques of 'Dark Alliance,' some of them on the front page, why would the *Post* not run his letter?"

Meanwhile, Webb received a tip from a reader that he should check the *Mercury News* archives from February 18,

1967. Webb went to the paper's library and found a reprint of a *Post* story written by Pincus: "How I Traveled Abroad on CIA Subsidy." In it, Pincus said a CIA recruiter approached him while he was a college student. The spook asked Pincus to spy on student groups at several international youth conferences in the late 1950s and early 1960s. Webb later wrote that he could hardly believe his eyes. The reporter who had been assigned to debunk his story—and who had the nerve to question his courtroom ethics—had collaborated with the CIA in spying operations? Webb could hardly contain his anger. "I'd certainly never spied on American citizens," he fumed.

Webb began researching Pincus and discovered that in 1975, he had written an unfavorable review of *CIA Diary*, a tell-all expose about the agency by ex-agent Philip Agee. Pincus had also covered the Iran contra affair, and had penned a story claiming that Special Prosecutor Lawrence Walsh was planning to indict Ronald Reagan, who at that point had just left office. In his memoirs, *Firewall*, Walsh claimed Pincus had been leaked that information in an attempt to discredit his investigation. "Of all the sideswipes that we suffered during this period, the false report that we were considering indicting the nation's still-admired former president hurt us the most," Walsh said.

In a recent interview, Pincus didn't deny his past relationship with the CIA, but claimed the only thing the agency did for him was pay his travel expenses to a 1959 youth conference in Vienna. "But I got to know a lot of people—some were friends," Pincus says. "I knew [former CIA director] George Tenet when he worked for John Heinz as a staffer on the [senate] intelligence committee, just as I knew

[Clinton Defense Secretary] Les Aspin when he was a young staffer for Bob McNamara. We were all young people in D.C. and went to a lot of dinners together."

While he acknowledges that his investigation confirmed that Blandon and Meneses had met with CIA asset Enrique Bermudez in Honduras, Pincus says such a meeting proves nothing. "It's a big leap to say that therefore the CIA, through one of its people, was arranging for drug deals to make money," he says. Pincus wouldn't have bothered responding to "Dark Alliance," he adds, but had no choice after the Congressional Black Caucus, led by Congresswoman Maxine Waters, began to make "a lot of noise" about the story. "A lot of people do intelligence stories that we don't report, because they are wrong," he says. "The thing that got me was the allegation that the CIA was responsible for bringing crack cocaine into South Central L.A.. That's off the wall."

NEXT TO JOIN the fray was the *Los Angeles Times*. On October 20, 1996, the paper published the first installment of an exhaustive three-day series that in its sheer length dwarfed "Dark Alliance." The first two days dealt directly with Webb's allegations while the final installment devoted countless speculative paragraphs to the question of whether African Americans were disproportionately likely to believe in conspiracy theories, something that did little to mend the paper's reputation for ignoring or belittling the concerns of the city's black population.

The *LA Times* also had to contend with the fact that

Webb had apparently scooped them on a story that had unfolded in the paper's own backyard. Editor Shelby Coffee III assigned more than two-dozen reporters to the story. The feeling among some disgruntled *LA Times* staffers was that their assignment wasn't to investigate "Dark Alliance," but debunk it. One of them told *New Times LA* that he had been selected to join the "Get Gary Webb Team," while another stated that a common remark among editors was, "We're going to take away this guy's Pulitzer."

Leo Wolinsky, then metro editor of the *LA Times*, helped to manage the paper's response. Now the paper's managing editor, Wolinsky says he'll never forget when he first read "Dark Alliance." "I remember having a knot in my stomach about it," he says. "It was a huge story—that the CIA started the crack binge in South Central L.A. That is an amazing allegation, and here in our area, it was like a smack in the face. It appeared convincing; it didn't appear to be garbage. You can't ignore a story like that in your backyard."

Leading the paper's response was Doyle McManus, the paper's Washington, D.C., bureau chief, who had covered the Iran contra scandal and had written several articles about the contras' alleged involvement with drug trafficking. McManus interviewed several CIA officials, including former CIA director Robert Gates, CIA agent Vincent Cannistraro, and current agency director John Deutch. Not surprisingly, all of them strongly denied that the agency had anything to do with drug smuggling. Like Pincus and Suro, McManus also failed to mention the 1986 Sheriff's department and DEA records Webb had cited in his story that flatly stated Blandon was still funding the

contras. "No solid evidence has emerged that either Meneses or Blandon contributed any money to the rebels after
1984," he surmised.

In a recent interview, McManus said his first reaction
upon reading "Dark Alliance" was that it demanded further
reporting. "Some parts sounded poorly sourced, but other
parts looked quite convincing, and all of it merited a serious
follow-up on our part," he says. "We had an obligation to do
our own reporting and to tell our readers whatever we found.
After further research, reporting, and interviews, I reached
the conclusion that most of the elements of the story that had
appeared new and significant on first reading were either not
new, not significant, or not supported by real evidence."

The most bizarre aspect of the paper's coverage was a
story by *LA Times* reporter Jesse Katz, the same reporter
who two years earlier had written that "Freeway" Ricky Ross
was the biggest crack dealer in the history of Los Angeles.
In 1994, Katz had estimated that at its peak, Ross' "coast-to-
coast conglomerate" was selling a half-million crack rocks per
day. "If there was an eye to the storm, if there was a criminal mastermind behind crack's decade-long reign, if there was
one outlaw capitalist most responsible for flooding Los
Angeles' streets with mass-marketed cocaine, his name was
"Freeway" Rick," Katz had written. "Ross did more than anyone else to democratize it, boosting volume, slashing prices,
and spreading disease on a scale never before conceived."

After Webb had revealed the source of much of that
cocaine to be a Nicaraguan contra sympathizer who had funneled some of his profits to the CIA-backed rebels, Katz had
a new take on Ross and his relative importance to the crack

plague. "The story of crack's genesis and evolution . . . is filled with a cast of interchangeable characters, from ruthless billionaires to strung-out curb dealers, none of whom is central to the drama," Katz wrote.

Now a reporter with *Los Angeles Magazine*, Katz says he was working at the *LA Times* bureau in Houston when he received a telephone call telling him to fly back to Los Angeles to help write a response to "Dark Alliance." It wasn't a task he particularly relished. "Is that something I wanted to do?" he asks. "No, it wasn't high on my list. There is something a little unseemly about having a major media institution dissect the work of another reporter."

Katz had met Webb while covering "Freeway" Ricky Ross' trial in San Diego, but had left the courtroom shortly after it began to work on another assignment. His only story about the trial was a brief article mentioning that Ross' lawyers planned to introduce evidence that the CIA had been involved in supplying him with drugs. At first, Katz says he felt that Webb had scooped him. "Gary had great journalistic instincts and terrific sense of dedication and doggedness, and I admired his willingness to dig, obviously to his own peril," Katz says. "But as I got sucked into this reviewing of his work and reviewing of my work and the whole crack epidemic, I began to feel there were parts of his series that were not as intellectually honest as they could have been or should have been."

When asked to explain the incongruity between his own reporting on Ross' relative importance in the city's crack trade before and after "Dark Alliance," Katz is somewhat at a loss for words. "I'm not sure I can answer that in a wholly satisfying way," he says. Referring to his 1994 story, Katz says he might have bought into the "mythology" surrounding Ross. "At the time, knowing people in the gang world and the drug enforcement world, he was the name that came up the most often and had a mythical quality," he says.

While Katz says his later story was an attempt to point out that the crack plague would have happened with or without Ross, he stands by his original assertion that Ross was L.A.'s first true crack kingpin. "He was at the front end of the crack wave," Katz says. "He was the first crack millionaire. He got rich doing this pretty much before everyone else in South Central got in on it."

Katz adds that his involvement with the mainstream media's critique of "Dark Alliance" has left many observers with the mistaken impression that he's an apologist for the CIA. "I don't put anything past the CIA, or think the CIA is going to tell the truth about what it does," he says. "They could be involved in any sort of thing. I know the *LA Times* wrote stories where the CIA was saying they didn't do anything. That wasn't my end of the coverage."

Just as happened with the original *Post* story, Webb's editors also defended him against the *LA Times* when the paper directly attacked not just the story, but Webb himself, in print. "One story that went over the wire from the *LA Times* included a paragraph that stated as fact that Gary and Ricky Ross had a movie deal together," says Garcia. "That was not true. What was true is that a movie agent had written up a movie deal contract, offered it to Ricky Ross and Gary—and Gary said no. That was sloppy reporting on the part of the *LA Times*. Just because Gary's name was printed on a contract did not mean he signed a contract for a movie deal. I called the *LA Times* city desk and told them they had an error in the story; it took a lot of convincing before they agreed to write a correction."

Garcia also got a telephone call from a reporter who asked if she could comment on the fact that Webb had shot at a man while he was a reporter at the *Kentucky Post*. Garcia was stunned, but calmly refused to comment until she checked with Webb. "Gary, did you shoot someone in [Kentucky] years ago?" she asked. "He said, yes, he did." Garcia held her breath while Webb explained how he confronted a thief trying to steal his car, and that the police hadn't pressed charges because he had acted in self-defense. To Garcia, the phone call suggested the media was digging for any piece of dirt on Gary, no matter how trivial or tangential, that would justify their attack of "Dark Alliance."

THE LAST OF the three major newspapers to pile on Webb's story was the *New York Times*. On October 21, 1996, the paper published a 1,536-word story, "Pivotal Figures of Newspaper Series May Be Only Bit Players" that, like the bulk of the reporting that preceded it, was based primarily on quotes from unnamed intelligence and law-enforcement officials. Reporter Tim Golden wrote that while both Blandon and Meneses "may indeed have provided modest support for the rebels, including perhaps some weapons, there is no evidence that either man was a rebel official or had anything to do with the CIA."

Adolfo Calero and other former contra leaders told

Golden that Meneses and Blandon had indeed met with CIA asset Enrique Bermudez in Honduras. But Golden noted that Webb had erroneously reported that Bermudez, a CIA operative, was an "agent," a mischaracterization apparently aimed at insinuating CIA complicity in his meeting with the two drug dealers. Golden also questioned Webb's assertion that Meneses served as chief of "intelligence and security" for the contras in California. Edward Navarro, a San Francisco contra organizer, recalled that Meneses showed up at some local contra meetings, but stood "quietly in the back." He claimed the only "security" operation the group undertook was to remove "the sign on their office door after protests by left-wing San Franciscans."

Golden found no evidence to indicate that the "relatively small amounts of cocaine" Blandon and Meneses "sometimes claimed to have brokered on behalf of the insurgents had a remotely significant role in the explosion of crack that began around the same time." His article acknowledged that "Freeway" Rick was "one of the biggest crack dealers in Los Angeles" but added, "several experts on the drug trade said that although Mr. Ross was indeed a crack kingpin, he was one of many."

Golden also wrote another—and much longer—story that ran in the *New York Times* that day, "Though Evidence is Thin, Tale of CIA and Drugs has a Life of its Own." Datelined from Compton, it began with Beverly Carr, a forty-eight-year-old African-American caterer who said she had always believed the CIA was behind the crack epidemic. "Everybody my age or older has always known that something like this was going on," she said. "Who down here in Watts or Compton has planes or boats to get these drugs up here? They're targeting the young black men. It's just ruining a whole generation."

Golden also questioned Webb's courtroom tactic of feeding questions to Ross' attorney, Alan Fenster. While Ceppos defended Webb on that score, he also identified—for the first time in print—what he considered a significant shortcoming in the story. "Were there things I would have done differently in retrospect?" Ceppos asked. "Yes. The principal thing I would have is one paragraph very high saying what we didn't find. We got to the door of the CIA. We did not get inside the CIA."

Unlike the *LA Times*, which had dozens of reporters assigned to the paper's examination of "Dark Alliance," Golden worked alone from the paper's San Francisco bureau, drawing on his personal knowledge of some of the terrain that Webb had covered in his story. Unlike McManus and Pincus, Golden hadn't reported on the Nicaraguan civil war mainly from a desk in Washington, but had been based in Central America and dealt extensively with the rebel leaders in Honduras and Costa Rica.

As a correspondent for the *Miami Herald*, Golden had written the first story exposing the contra's use of the Salvadoran air force base at Ilopango as a re-supply center. Other stories probed corruption among contra officials, primarily on Eden Pastora's so-called Southern Front, and allegations of human rights violations by various contra factions. He shared in a Pulitzer Prize awarded to the *Herald* for its coverage of events leading up to the Iran contra scandal. Despite assertions to the contrary by some of Webb's more venomous defenders,

Golden can hardly be considered a CIA dupe. Now an investigative reporter for the *New York Times*, his recent work has exposed abuses by U.S. soldiers and intelligence operatives in Afghanistan, Iraq, and Guantanamo Bay, Cuba.

Looking back at his own story, Golden now concedes that it appears "a little credulous of the intelligence and contra sources" who denied any complicity with drug trafficking, although most critics of the media reaction to "Dark Alliance" found it more measured than that of the *LA Times*. "I'm not sure it was the deepest reporting we ever did," Golden says. "But it was not hard to find big journalistic holes in Webb's series."

Although his first reaction to Webb's story was that it was "interesting," Golden felt that Webb had "clearly overreached" in his conclusion that Blandon and Meneses, or even the contras in general, had contributed much to the booming drug trade. Despite allegations that contra leaders had lined their own pockets with CIA and State Department funds, the contra troops that Golden had seen in the field in the mid-1980s did not appear to have been especially well-armed or well-provisioned.

Golden also found it hard to stomach the outrage over Webb's "unproven" claim that the contra war had helped fuel the crack epidemic. "It was by then pretty clear that the contras had tortured or murdered hundreds and probably thousands of Nicaraguans," Golden says. "Americans didn't care a whole lot about the fact that their government had paid for that. But because some contra hangers-on had moved a relatively small amount of drugs, people were in an uproar. I thought it was the height of American narcissism."

While he does not question that elements of the contras

were involved in drugs, Golden's view is that they were almost all minor players who were peripheral to the rebel armies. "Compared to the number of guys who were pulling out fingernails, I don't think drug-dealing was that high on the list of the bad things they were doing," he says. "It was interesting that a couple of Nicaraguan exiles had hooked up with this big crack dealer, but the central premise of [Webb's] story—that the contra war and its funding needs fueled the crack epidemic—there is still to this day nothing solid that makes this case."

Some years after reporting from Central America, Golden had covered the drug trade in Mexico and Colombia. Webb's assertion that Ross was the kingpin of crack reminded him of the way the DEA hyped the arrests of major coke traffickers. As was already obvious at that time, one smuggler replaced another, he says. "The idea that one guy was the king of all wholesale crack deals in South Central did not fit with my understanding of how the drug trade worked."

Golden came to the conclusion that Webb and his defenders did not care much about getting to the truth of the story—they just wanted the story to be true. He recalls debating Webb and other journalists at a 1997 Society of Professional Journalists panel in San Francisco. "I had by then spent ten years of my life writing about the bad things that our government and others had done in Latin America, and I practically got booed out of the room as some kind of apologist," he says.

Shortly after his *New York Times* story appeared, protesters from various groups, including the San Francisco-based activist group Global Exchange, picketed outside his office.

Golden went downstairs and, without introducing himself, infiltrated the protest. He chatted with the demonstrators as they denounced him as a tool of the CIA. "People had too much time on their hands in those days," he says. "It was a time when journalism and politics were a little unmoored, as if people didn't know who the real enemy was . . . I don't think it was a high-water mark for investigative journalism."

WEBB HAD HIS defenders, especially in the alternative press. Fairness and Accuracy in Reporting published a lengthy, well-reasoned critique of the mainstream media's attack against "Dark Alliance," calling it a "Snow Job." But the most eloquent pundit to jump to Webb's aid was Alexander Cockburn, who later co-authored a book with investigative reporter Jeffrey St. Clair, *White Out: The CIA, Drugs and The Press*, a detailed history of agency collusion with drug traffickers and the media's failure to cover the story. Cockburn says the mainstream media's attacks against Webb constituted the most "factually inane" feeding frenzy he's ever witnessed, but that it didn't particularly surprise him.

"I've never taken the view that the mainstream press in the U.S. is to be redeemed," Cockburn says. "The rhetorical pose is always that the *New York Times* could be doing a better job and so could the *Washington Post* and then we would have a responsible press. My view is that the official corporate press is there to do a bad job. That's its function and nobody should be surprised. The miracle is that the *Mercury News* was asleep at the wheel and didn't realize what Webb was doing—and printed his story.

Other alternative journalists were less forgiving of the flaws in "Dark Alliance," but equally skeptical of the mainstream media's criticism of the story. "If Gary Webb made mistakes I have no problem with exposing them," says *LA Weekly's* Marc Cooper. "But given the sweep of American journalism over the past fifty years, this is an outstanding case where three of the major newspapers in the country just decided to take out a competitor whose mistakes seem by any measure to be very minor."

Cooper has special scorn for the *LA Times'* Doyle McManus, whom he accuses of routinely authoring stories about Nicaragua that were spun from Reagan Administration lies, and which helped the U.S. government build support for the contras. "The stories that Doyle McManus wrote about Nicaragua in the 1980s—and the stories that [disgraced *New York Times* reporter] Judy Miller wrote about weapons of mass destruction in Iraq twenty years later— those are high crimes," Cooper says. "Those are stories where reporters speak to officials based on anonymity and the stories are false; they have no substance."

McManus says it was his job to quote anonymous sources. "I did not trust official denials," he says. "I reported denials when officials made them in response to accusations, but that doesn't mean I trusted them. I believed, and still believe, that people in the U.S. government turned a blind eye to drug dealing by people connected with the contras. I reported those allegations beginning in 1987, and I included them in our 1996 story about 'Dark Alliance.'"

David Corn, Washington Editor of the *Nation* magazine, reported extensively on the contra-drug connection during the 1980s. When he first read "Dark Alliance," Corn says he was impressed that Webb had found "street-level" sources on what appeared to be a major U.S. drug ring funding the Nicaraguan contras. But he quickly realized the story didn't support its dramatic conclusion that the CIA or the contras had sparked the crack-cocaine epidemic. Yet Corn also believes the mainstream media, which had always ignored the contra-drug story, failed just as dramatically in its own response to "Dark Alliance."

"What they did, particularly the *LA Times* and *Washington Post*, was to jump all over 'Dark Alliance' without looking at the bigger issue of connections between the CIA-backed contras and drug dealing," Corn says. The coverage brought Corn back to the afternoon in 1987 when he attended a Capitol Hill press conference where officials unveiled the U.S. Senate's final Iran contra report.

"One reporter in the room, a freelancer, asked if they had investigated the allegations of contra drug running," Corn recalls. "And a reporter for the *New York Times* said, 'Come on, let's talk about something serious.' Those of us who followed this closely, and it was just a small number of reporters, knew there was a story here to which the mainstream press had never paid serious attention. Then when Gary Webb's story came along, they were happy to jump on that and shoot it down without examining their own failings on that front."

One of the few people who had followed the contra drug story, Corn says, is Peter Kornbluh, director of the Cuba Documentation Project and Chile Documentation Project at the National Security Archives at George Washington

University. Like Corn and others, Kornbluh believes Webb over-reached with his reporting by suggesting that the Blandon-Meneses-Ross network played a significant role in America's crack epidemic. He also believes the main-stream media was motivated less by the errors in Webb's work than by the firestorm of controversy they produced, and that the one-sidedness of their reaction was journalistically indefensible.

"I thought the reaction particularly of the *LA Times*, but also of the two other papers was one of the most wasteful expenditures of journalistic resources in the recent history of journalism," Kornbluh says. "I've never seen anything like it in thirty years. If that much energy, particularly by the *LA Times*, had been expended on the true scandal of con-tras and drugs, Gary's reporting would have been signifi-cantly expanded."

Of the three major newspapers that criticized "Dark Alliance," only the *Washington Post* later saw fit to question its own coverage. On November 10, 1996, a few weeks after the anti-Webb onslaught had subsided, *Washington Post* ombudsman Geneva Overholser excoriated Webb for "Dark Alliance's" shortcomings, but acknowledged the unseemliness of the mainstream media's feeding frenzy, which she deemed "misplaced."

"A principal responsibility of the press is to protect the people from government excesses," Overholser argued. "The *Post* (among others) showed more energy for protecting the CIA from someone else's journalistic excesses . . . Would that we had welcomed the surge of public interest as an occasion to return to a subject the *Post* and the public had given short shrift. Alas, dismissing someone else's story as old news comes more naturally."

A decade of hindsight, however, has softened the perspective of many of the journalists that attacked Gary Webb in print. Ironically, because his newspaper was the most aggressive in criticizing "Dark Alliance," Leo Wolinsky of the *LA Times* says he wishes Webb had worked for him. "The truth is that, with a good editor, it would have been a great story," Wolinsky says. "I could see that story in the *LA Times* in draft form; it just needed an editor who would ask the right questions. In some ways Gary got too much blame. He did exactly what you expect from a great investigative reporter."

Mea Culpa

NINE

DESPITE THE BARRAGE of criticism against "Dark Alliance" in the nation's largest and most respected newspapers, Gary Webb had every reason to think that his editors would stand by him. Executive editor Jerry Ceppos had defended Webb in interviews with the *New York Times*, *LA Times*, and *Washington Post*, and even had written a trenchant letter to the editor about the latter paper's coverage of his story.

When other reporters at the *Mercury News* who weren't happy about the controversy openly groused about Webb, Ceppos posted a memo on an editorial bulletin board asking them to keep their views to themselves. At a staff party at the paper, he had jauntily displayed his courage under fire by donning a military helmet.

Webb wanted to go on the offensive against his critics. He suggested stories about Walter Pincus' ties to the CIA and how the *LA Times* had known about the 1986 raids against the Blandon ring—and had even obtained information about the evidence seized in Ronald Lister's house—but had chosen not to report it. "The best way to shut them up is to put the rest of what we know in the paper and keep plowing ahead," Webb later said he told Ceppos.

Yet it wasn't just Webb's credibility that was being questioned, but that of the *Mercury News* itself. Ceppos was in no mood to print stories attacking other newspapers. He wanted to print a written response to their criticism, but wasn't sure Webb was the man to do it. Instead, Ceppos appointed the paper's most experienced investigative reporter, Pete Carey, and an L.A. bureau reporter, Pamela Kramer, to write follow-up articles. Carey worked on his own from the paper's headquarters in San Jose, while Kramer and Webb teamed up for field assignments in Southern California. Ceppos also gave Webb permission to return to Central America to gather more evidence to bolster his story.

While Webb was in Costa Rica interviewing new sources, Carey and Kramer were writing follow-up stories about the controversy. "My role was to do the community follow-ups," says Kramer, who later left the *Mercury News* to pursue a teaching career. "Clearly the response was stratospherically greater from the public than what the *Mercury* had prepared for. It ranged from legitimate community interest to people getting CIA signals in their heads. I got a lot of those calls because I was listed in the L.A. directory for the *Mercury News*."

Kramer had seen Webb around the office when she worked as an intern at the *Cleveland Plain Dealer*, but had never spoken to him until she accompanied him on several reporting gigs in L.A. The pair interviewed the Sheriff's deputies who had raided the Blandon drug ring in 1986, and even knocked on the door of Lister's vacant Mission Viejo house. Kramer recalls that there was tin foil in all the windows.

"I was sent to team report, ostensibly for two reasons," Kramer says. " One was that I had requested to work with an investigative reporter a year earlier, but also because I was a 'solid person.' It was not that Dawn [Garcia] was casting any aspersions on Gary but she was saying because of the controversy that was surrounding him, they wanted a second set of eyes there. It was not that I was being a spy; it was team reporting. And it was cool. It was fun."

Kramer's first impression of "Dark Alliance" was that the story made for breathtaking reading but seemed a bit grandiose—at least that's how she felt when she saw the phrase "crack-cocaine explosion" in the lead paragraph. But more to the point, she felt amazed that nobody had told her the story was in the works, given that she was the paper's L.A. correspondent. "This was in my backyard and I didn't know anything about it," she says. "Nobody said anything about it."

After one assignment in Los Angeles, Kramer drove Webb to the airport, so he could catch his flight to San Diego. While Webb retrieved his belongings from a locker, Kramer waited for him on the departures level. After ten minutes, Webb hadn't returned. "I was about to get out of the car and give ten bucks to this guy on a bench and give him a description of Gary," Kramer says. At that moment, a police officer knocked on her window. "The cop says, 'Hey, is your name by any chance, Pam? There is a guy downstairs who's convinced you've been kidnapped.'" As it turned out, Webb had gone downstairs to the arrivals lane. "He thought the CIA had me," Kramer says.

Webb flew to Costa Rica, where he and freelancer Georg Hodel interviewed police and prosecutors about Meneses and his connection to contra activities there. Hodel located Carlos Cabezas, a contra pilot who claimed he had delivered millions of dollars in drug funds to the contras. Cabezas, whom DEA reports show was involved with Meneses' drug ring, claimed that he was taking orders from a CIA agent in Costa Rica named Ivan Gomez. Hodel also tracked down Enrique Miranda, who had testified against Meneses during the latter's trial in Nicaragua on drug charges. Miranda told Hodel that Meneses had long operated with CIA protection.

Back in California after the trip, Webb began typing up his findings, convinced that they would settle the question of Blandon and Meneses ties to the CIA once and for all. Besides the new information he had unearthed in California, Webb had 3,000 pages of records released by the L.A. County Sheriff's Department about the agency's 1986 raids on the Blandon-Ross network—documents that further bolstered his assertion that Blandon was still funding the contras with drug money several years after he and Meneses met CIA asset Enrique Bermudez in Honduras.

Webb felt jubilant. "We'd done it," he later recalled. "I expected the editors to be besides themselves with joy." Instead, nothing happened. "Aside from Dawn, no one called me to tell me they'd read the new stories," Webb later wrote. "No one called with questions. No one even suggested that we begin editing them."

What Webb didn't know was that Pete Carey, whom Ceppos had assigned to investigate the controversy over "Dark Alliance" while Kramer was busy reporting on the black community's reaction, had spent weeks trying to advance Webb's story, and had come up empty handed. Carey's job was to do nothing short of vindicate "Dark Alliance" from the attacks it had suffered at the hands of the nation's most powerful newspapers.

In a recent interview, Carey said he got the assignment after approaching Ceppos in October 1996, at the height of the media's criticism of the story. "I remember walking into Jerry's office and saying, 'Boy, we need to do a story on this,'" Carey says. "We are really taking a beating." Carey convinced Ceppos it was imperative for the paper to acknowledge in print that the *Mercury News* had been subjected to unprecedented criticism by the nation's leading newspapers. "We owe it to our readers," he told Ceppos.

When Ceppos gave Carey the job of investigating Webb's story, the idea was that if anybody could ferret out the truth, Carey could. After all, Carey had covered Iran contra for Knight Ridder News Service and knew the basic terrain of the story. If he found that Webb was right, Ceppos reasoned, perhaps the newspapers that attacked "Dark Alliance" would admit they had wrongly maligned the *Mercury News*.

But while Carey says he went into his investigation hoping to advance the story, he quickly determined it would not be easy. The first inkling Carey had that something was wrong was when he looked at Blandon's trial transcripts.

Webb had reported that Blandon's testimony showed he had been dealing drugs for the contras for "the better part of a decade." Instead, Carey wasn't sure what the transcripts showed. "There were important, contradictory statements that didn't make it into the series," Carey says. "It was kind of disheartening. I am a firm believer in telling the whole story, in laying out the weaknesses as well as the strengths. There was a lot of ambiguity."

Ultimately, Carey came to roughly the same conclusion that the *Post*'s Walter Pincus and other reporters who had examined Blandon's testimony had reached: by the time Blandon began dealing coke to "Freeway" Ricky Ross, he had broken with Meneses and was no longer sending cash to support the contras. While that was a reasonable conclusion, based on a fair reading of Blandon's testimony, it ignored the L.A. County Sheriff's Department's 1986 report saying Blandon's drug proceeds were still being funneled to the contras four years after Blandon started supplying Ross with coke.

When Carey confronted Webb about the contradiction in Blandon's testimony, he says Webb told him Blandon was lying when he tried to downplay the length of time he dealt drugs for the contras. But "Dark Alliance" had specifically asserted that Blandon had sent "millions" of dollars worth of drug funds to the contras, and Carey could find no proof for that claim. "This thing about millions of dollars—it looked like an error of exaggeration," Carey says. "How could something like that get inflated? You start with two drug dealers who were completely untrustworthy. I mean, find me a drug dealer who doesn't claim he's in the CIA."

Carey made scores of phone calls in the course of his investigation, including one to contra leader Adolfo Calero. "It's nice to finally hear from someone at the *Mercury News*," Calero joked. Carey asked Calero about the photograph of him and Meneses together at a meeting in San Francisco. Calero said he didn't remember meeting Meneses, because he had been to countless contra fundraising meetings. Carey had less luck tracking down Ivan Gomez, the mysterious CIA agent Cabezas had said directed Meneses' drug pipeline. At one point, Carey heard that Gomez may have moved to Venezuela, but there were dozens of people with the same name living there.

Although Carey had no way of knowing it, the task was pointless. As the CIA would admit in its 1998 Inspector General report, Ivan Gomez was actually a pseudonym used by a CIA agent assigned to Costa Rica in the 1980s.

Carey could also find scant evidence to support the notion that Blandon's supply of coke to Ross had "fueled" L.A.'s crack epidemic, despite the fact that Ross was the city's most notorious crack dealer. Getting confirmation for that assertion was perhaps Carey's prime directive from his editor, Jonathan Krim. Carey called thirty cocaine experts, and none of them agreed that Ross had played a critical role in either crack cocaine's origins or its eventual spread throughout the country.

"What we were left with was a more nuanced view of what started the crack epidemic," Carey says. "The three major premises of the story looked a little shaky. It seemed like a reasonable thing to set the record straight while not completely backing away from the story. You still had a fascinating story about these two dealers peddling to Ross, the beginning of the crack epidemic at least in L.A. All this is impressive stuff, gripping narrative, but the rest lacked substantiation. That's great for a novel, but where's the evidence?"

In early February 1997, Dawn Garcia sent Webb a draft of the story Carey had written on the emergence of L.A.'s crack market. The story stated that Blandon, Meneses, and Ross could not have single-handedly started the crack-cocaine explosion. "The details of the trio's activities—who did what, and when—cannot change the overall story of the crack epidemic, which swept over several U.S. cities in the mid-1980s with the speed and destruction of a tidal wave," Carey concluded.

Webb felt betrayed. "It was, astonishingly, a virtual repeat of the *LA Times* stories," he later recalled. "I couldn't believe it. I respected Carey as a reporter—he and I had coau-thored a story in 1989 that had won a Pulitzer Prize. But here it seemed he'd taken the official government explana-tion and swallowed it hook, line, and sinker."

Over the next several weeks, Webb met with Carey, Gar-cia, Krim, and Ceppos, and argued about what the *Mercury News* should do with the result of Carey's investigation. In the end, they decided not to print Carey's story, opting instead for a high profile letter to readers written by Ceppos himself.

Krim says he was saddened by the results of Carey's work. "Given the beating we were taking, nothing would have pleased me more than to be able to report back, to our executive editor, to our publisher, and most importantly to our readers, that we could stand by the story," he says. "I came as close as a non-religious man can come to praying for that outcome. Alas, the results of our re-examination were profoundly disturbing."

Although Krim had wished for stronger direct evidence of the links between the CIA and the drug ring, he was generally satisfied that a relationship existed between the agency and some of the drug dealers, and that some of the money was helping contra efforts. "Gary had gotten closer to documenting it than anyone could have been expected to," he says. "And that's a damn good story. There were some errors in the piece which were used to bludgeon us, but in my view they did not undermine the basic premise."

If any evidence had been produced to undermine the attacks on "Dark Alliance," Krim insists he would happily have printed it. He bristles at the notion that he or other editors simply buckled under the pressure of media attacks when it backed away from the story. "Nothing pisses me off and offends me more than to read about how *Mercury News* management was just cowering in the corner, looking for a way out and only too happy to sacrifice Gary Webb to find one," he says.

As Ceppos pondered his next move, Webb went back to work, trying to salvage "Dark Alliance." In March, he flew to Miami and interviewed a former CIA pilot named Ronald Lippert, who had delivered weapons to the contras. Lippert told Webb that he had helped the DEA fly John Hull—the expatriate American contra supporter Martha Honey had investigated in Honduras a decade earlier—out of Costa Rica. In an interview with Webb, Hull confirmed the story.

"I was ecstatic," Webb later recalled. "Now we had a

story about the DEA aiding and abetting the escape of a CIA agent accused of drug trafficking, with the Justice Department intervening to protect the DEA agent who'd done it," he wrote. But in January 1997, when Webb shared his discoveries with Garcia, she didn't respond.

Garcia says that when she saw the results of Webb's latest research about Hull's escape from Costa Rica, she realized his latest work did little to answer the story's critics. "We [had] talked numerous times, but I was having a hard time getting a clear read what Gary was getting from his reporting," she says. "When I read the drafts of the four follow-up stories Gary filed, my heart sank. What he came back with was a totally different story. It was mostly about the DEA, which was related and interesting, but it would not answer our critics. All of his editors who read his four stories thought, 'Oh, no; this is not going to do it.' It was the beginning of the end."

On March 25, Ceppos called Webb at home to announce that he had made a "very difficult decision." The newspaper was going to print a letter to its readers acknowledging that "errors had been made in Webb's story." Ceppos faxed Webb a draft of what he proposed to write. The column stated that the *Mercury News* should have pointed out that Blandon had claimed he stopped dealing drugs with the contras in 1983, that there was "insufficient proof" that millions of dollars went to support the rebels, that the story lacked direct evidence of CIA knowledge of the drug dealing, and that Blandon, Meneses, and Ross didn't start the crack epidemic.

According to Garcia, Ceppos felt like he had been supporting Webb all along, and that Webb had misled him about his research in Central America. "The stories Gary filed weren't what we asked him to do," Garcia says. "That was hard. Gary, meanwhile, felt like he was being hung out to dry. I don't know if Gary thought his stories would silence our critics; he seemed very excited about what he had, but I think deep down he had to know that it was not directly on point, or what the editors asked for. Perhaps he didn't care; he thought it was good."

Webb drove to San Jose to meet with his editors. He was incensed, in part because an earlier draft of his story had included the fact that Blandon claimed he stopped providing drug money to the contras in 1983, but Garcia had agreed with him that Blandon was probably lying— and cut the quote to save space. In his 1998 book, Webb wrote that he agreed there were "mistakes" in the story. "But this draft doesn't mention them," he said. "If we want to fully air this issue and be honest with our readers, I request that the following 'failures' be included."

In his meeting with Ceppos, Webb listed those errors: how it was his editors, chiefly Yarnold, who had requested more emphasis on CIA ties to the Blandon-Meneses drug ring, how cutting the series from four parts to three had trashed the kind of nuance they were now claiming was essential, and how the last-minute change in editors from Yarnold to Paul Van Slambrouck had further confused the story. Webb demanded that the *Mercury News* print his response to the letter to readers they planned to run.

Ceppos told Webb he didn't want the situation to become "personal," but that didn't stop Webb from going on the radio to denounce what he saw as a cowardly betrayal. "I don't know why Gary didn't understand that publicly berating your own paper isn't going to help you, but maybe he was so mad, he couldn't help himself," Garcia says. "Ceppos was quoted as saying what Gary filed was just notes. While it was more than notes, the stories would have needed some very serious editing, even if they were on point. Gary said the paper was refusing to run his stories that would have vindicated him. But if Gary had found anything that would have answered our critics, we surely would have run it."

Ceppos' mea culpa ran on May 11, 1997—and over Webb's objections, did not include his response. Although it acknowledged significant errors in "Dark Alliance," it also defended many aspects of Webb's reporting. "Does the presence of conflicting information invalidate our entire effort?" he asked. "I strongly believe the answer is no, and that this story was right on many important points."

Although the column hardly represented a total retraction of the story, that's how it was it universally received—something Webb had predicted would happen. Mike Mansfield, the CIA's public affairs director, was positively ecstatic about Ceppos' column. "It is gratifying to see that a large segment of the media—including the *San Jose Mercury News* itself—has taken a serious and objective look at how this story was reported," Mansfield told me in a 1997 interview. The reaction among the papers that had criticized "Dark Alliance" was equally self-congratulatory. All three major newspapers ran front-page stories on the event. "The *Mercury News* Comes Clean," stated a patronizing editorial in the *New York Times*.

Garcia says that the media's reaction also included

personal attacks against everyone involved in the story, including her and Ceppos. "In one *Columbia Journalism Review* article in July 1997, the story mentioned my recent divorce and described me as a 'young Latina,' as if those pieces of information had bearing on the series," she says.

But those barbs were mild compared to the media's attempts to eviscerate Webb's credibility. A few weeks after Ceppos published his column, *Times* reporter Iver Peterson wrote a scathing critique of Webb's entire career that focused on the lawsuits during his tenure at the *Plain Dealer* and the complaints of unfairness over his *Mercury News* story about Tandem Computers, while ignoring his many accomplishments. "The controversy . . . has drawn additional scrutiny to Mr. Webb, whose bare-knuckles reporting style and penchant for self-promotion have drawn criticism not only from his targets, but also from his colleagues," Peterson wrote.

At a journalist's conference several months after that story appeared, Webb's former colleague at the *Plain Dealer*, Walt Bogdanich, now a *New York Times* editor, denounced Peterson's story in a panel discussion. "That article included virtually none of the good things Gary did," Bogdanich says. "It didn't include the success he achieved, or the wrongs that he righted—and they were considerable. It wasn't fair, and it made him out to be a freak."

At the event, Bogdanich bumped into Webb, whom he didn't realize was there. "He seemed changed," Bogdanich says. "There didn't seem to be much laughter with him anymore. He wasn't the guy I remembered, and understandably so: he was being put through a meat-grinder." Webb thanked his former colleague for his remarks; the two never spoke again.

In Nicaragua, the right-wing press celebrated the news that the *Mercury News* had repudiated Webb's story. Georg Hodel, the Swiss reporter who had helped Webb research the story, received numerous threats. In June, he was run off the road by a group of armed men. Fearing for his life, he ultimately fled the country. Hodel could not be located for an interview.

Meanwhile, Webb told reporters that he was "disgusted" by the column. "But what's even more disgusting is the fact that the establishment press is using this to absolve the CIA of any wrongdoing," he told me in a 1997 interview. "Gary was furious," Carey recalls. "He was clearly veering away from the paper. He was like, 'Go ahead and fire me.' I don't think he quite got what was happening until he read Ceppos' column. That really flipped him out."

Webb believed he was being censored—he had written four follow-up stories that advanced his reporting and his editors were refusing to publish them. Joe Madison, the Washington, D.C., talk show host, told his listeners to call the *Mercury News* and demand they run the stories. The alternative press universally hailed Webb as a scapegoat, attacking Ceppos for caving in to corporate pressure. More paranoid observers on the Internet surmised that Ceppos was taking his orders from the CIA itself.

French TV journalist Paul Moreira flew to California and interviewed Webb shortly after Ceppos published his mea culpa. Moreira had covered the civil war in Nicaragua in 1989, and was arrested and nearly executed by a contra

patrol near Jinotega, Nicaragua. "The contras were ferocious," Moreira says. "I was amazed by the quality of their
equipment. Sandinistas soldiers looked like bums compared to them."

When Moreira interviewed Webb, he noticed that his colleagues didn't seem happy about the media attention. "They
didn't want to him to keep defending himself, obviously," he
says. "I had come to do a story because I could see the core
of his work was true. I had seen the evidence, the documents. I felt it was unfair that he would be bashed like that."

Another source of contention between Webb and his
editors was the fact that several major publishers were offering Webb handsome offers for a book. But Ceppos told
Webb he'd have to quit his job if he wanted to write a book.
Sue recalls that Webb had one offer from Simon & Schus-
ter that would have paid at least $100,000. "That's what he
should have done," she says. "But Gary still had total loyalty
to the paper. I didn't feel like I could change his mind."

Webb's loyalty to the *Mercury News*, and his decision to
forgo lucrative book deals to remain with the paper, only
fueled his defensive and outspoken reaction once his editors
backed off his big story. "Gary's fate after 'Dark Alliance' was
determined not by his work, but by his actions during the re-
examination and after," says Jonathan Krim. Webb simply
didn't respond to criticism well. "He often responded to concerns not with reasoned argument, but with accusations of
us selling him out," he says. "Under those circumstances,
how could editors be expected to trust Gary on any sensitive reporting subject?"

Garcia says she felt bad for Webb, but also felt he had

been his own worst enemy. "As awful as I felt about what Gary was going through, both inside the newsroom and outside, in the end, I felt somewhat betrayed by Gary," she says. "I had worked hard to help him make this series work. As his editor, I had been his main advocate and also tried to save him from his worst instincts, painstakingly going over all his evidence with him for each point he made in the series, again and again."

But in the end, Garcia says she came to believe there was contradictory information Webb had gathered in his reporting that he hadn't told her about—chiefly the inconsistencies in Blandon's testimony. "When I asked him about it, he said he didn't think it was important," Garcia says. "Had I known everything he knew, I think I could have helped him craft a story that would have been just as important but more nuanced. It would not have drawn the sweeping conclusions it did, conclusions that we could not ultimately support in every way."

In early June, Ceppos called Webb with an ultimatum. He'd have to accept a reassignment at the paper's headquarters in San Jose, where he'd work under closer supervision, or as specified in his employment contract, he could go to a smaller regional bureau in Cupertino. After talking to Sue, Webb took the offer to work in Cupertino, the journalistic equivalent of a news graveyard, and a major demotion. Sue recalls the day Webb left as the saddest moment in his life. "That crushed him," she says. "He was crying when he left that night. He felt like he was being taken away from his family."

Webb's oldest son, Ian, says his father's transfer to the

paper marked the first time he realized his dad was depressed. He had seen how hard his father had worked on "Dark Alliance," how he had spent weeks and even months away from the family. "Now he was getting slammed for all this stuff that people didn't want to believe," Ian says. "That definitely made him depressed. It made everybody depressed. I went from having a dad on a daily basis to seeing him on weekends. It sucked."

Webb moved into a furnished apartment in Cupertino, more than 150 miles away from Sue and his three kids. Instead of working on major investigative stories, he was assigned to cover the daily blotter of traffic accidents and lost puppies—the kind of work he'd done two decades earlier as a cub reporter in Kentucky. Webb refused to have his byline run in the paper. His first story was about a police horse that died from constipation. Meanwhile, he continued to fight his transfer through the newspaper's union guild.

"It was pretty miserable living in a motel room," Webb told author Charles Bowden in 1998. "I was getting really depressed. They were stringing me out on this [arbitration] hearing. Finally, I just started calling Sue. I was very angry most of the time. I was waking up in the middle of the night." In August, Webb began calling in sick after talking to a doctor who diagnosed him with severe depression. "She said you are under a great deal of stress; the environment you are living in isn't healthy," Webb told Bowden. "It was a lot worse than I realized until I started going to someone and talking about it . . . I just felt like I'd come to the end of the line."

After several months of writing stories that meant

absolutely nothing to him, and commuting back to Sacramento every weekend, he ran out of reasons to stay at the paper. "Gary didn't like to back down," Sue says. "But he was tired of fighting." On November 19, 1997, he tendered his formal resignation from the *Mercury News*. Webb told Bowden that he carried the resignation letter in his briefcase for weeks before he signed it. "Writing my name on that thing meant the end of my career," he said. "I saw it as some sort of a surrender. It was like signing my . . . death certificate."

After twenty years in journalism and just over a year after the publication of the biggest story of his life, Gary Webb suddenly found himself unemployed.

Lister TEN

LESS THAN A week after the *Mercury News* formally announced Gary Webb's resignation, the CIA released its official response to "Dark Alliance." Although a declassified version of the report hadn't yet been made public, the agency leaked an executive summary to the *Los Angeles Times*, the newspaper that had been the most critical of Webb's story.

"CIA Probe Absolves Agency on L.A. Crack," read the triumphal headline of a December 18 story by *LA Times* writers Doyle McManus and James Risen. "The CIA has completed a report declaring it was not responsible for introducing crack cocaine to Los Angeles." But a careful reading of the story revealed that the CIA's Inspector General failed to question numerous former agents involved in the agency's support of the Nicaraguan contras. Although McManus and Risen characterized the report as the most "intensive" in the history of the CIA, agency investigators had no authority to force anyone to talk.

One former CIA officer admitted the agency had interviewed him "simply to go through all the motions of touching all the bases." Former CIA officer Duane R. Clarridge, who ran the agency's covert war against the Sandinistas, refused to answer any questions, and told the *LA Times* he wrote the CIA a letter describing its investigation as "bullshit." Pete Carey covered the release of the report for the *Mercury News*. His story reported that CIA investigators had argued with a witness who claimed the CIA knew about drug trafficking by people the agency had used on various assignments. "You guys don't want to know the truth," Carey quoted the witness as telling the CIA.

While the early news accounts of the CIA's self-vindication got front-page treatment in the nation's major newspapers, the actual report, released a month later, just as the media began obsessing over the Monica Lewinsky scandal, did not. Although the bulk of the report contained nothing to directly vindicate "Dark Alliance," the CIA acknowledged for the first time that the agency had intervened in the infamous Frogman case of January 1983, when a group of Nicaraguan traffickers were arrested shortly after unloading 430 pounds of cocaine from a Colombian freighter in the waters off San Francisco.

A year after the arrests, the CIA asked the Justice Department to return $36,800 that had been seized from the traffickers. The cash, the CIA argued, wasn't drug money, but funds intended for the contras. In its report, the agency claimed it did this "to protect an operational equity, i.e., a contra support group in which it had an operational interest." CIA lawyers asked the federal prosecutor handling the Frogman case not to report their request, because "there are sufficient factual details which would cause certain damage to our image and program in Central America."

The leader of the drug ring—according to law enforcement records Webb had uncovered—was none other than Norwin Meneses. The DEA never charged Meneses in the scheme, however, and the portion of the CIA report dealing with the Frogman case didn't mention his tie to the smuggling operation.

Shortly after the CIA released its 1998 report, the Justice Department's Inspector General published the results of its investigation, which also cleared the CIA of wrongdoing. "Meneses was investigated several times over the course of many years," the report stated. "Some of his associates were successfully prosecuted, although the DEA never obtained sufficient evidence to prosecute Meneses. Contrary to the *Mercury News* claims, we did not find that these investigations were halted because of any alleged connection between Meneses and the Contras or the CIA."

The Justice Department also stated that while Blandon was a major trafficker, it found no evidence that he had provided "substantial" drug money to support the contras. Of Blandon's associate, Ronald Lister, the report stated that while the documents seized at his home in 1986 "largely corroborate his account that he was seeking to sell military and security equipment and weaponry to the Contras and factions in El Salvador," the agency had "found no evidence that he was successful in this venture."

Investigators did uncover an FBI memo concerning an informant who overheard Lister bragging over drinks that he worked for Oliver North, who directed the Reagan administration's secret contra arms-supply network. Although the Justice Department said it found no evidence to support or contradict that claim, an "Operation Homeport" code sheet found among North's notes shows that, perhaps coincidentally, he typed the word "Lister" as the code word for "advisers"—on a list that includes code words for everything from "missiles" and "grenades" to "Lebanon" and "hostages."

The report also revealed that the FBI investigated Lister's various arms deals at least five times between 1983 and 1986. In September 1983, the FBI probed Lister for illegally selling weapons to El Salvador and "other countries," and for arranging covert loans from Saudi Arabia to the Salvadoran government. Without elaborating on the specifics of those deals, the Justice Department simply concluded that none of the investigations bolstered Lister's claim of CIA affiliation. "We did not find that he had any such affiliation," the report stated. "Rather, such comments were part of a pattern of deception that Lister engaged in for years when attempting to shield his illegal activities."

THERE'S MUCH MORE to Lister's story than the Justice Department, the newspapers that criticized "Dark Alliance," or the CIA itself would care to admit, however. As an investigative reporter for *OC Weekly*, I spent months digging into Lister and his claim of CIA affiliation. While it was clear Lister was a habitual liar and eventually a coke addict, his friends and business contacts included former CIA officials and covert operatives who were active in Central America and elsewhere during the 1980s. These strange—and to Webb's critics, rather inconvenient—relationships were never adequately answered by the Justice Department or CIA, which to this day have refused to release uncensored copies of their files on Lister because of "national security" concerns—an odd claim assuming Lister had no involvement with matters of national security.

In its response to "Dark Alliance," the *LA Times* dismissed Lister as a "con artist," and quoted Lister's employee, Christopher Moore, who had traveled to El Salvador with Lister, saying he didn't believe "nine-tenths" of what Lister told him. The paper also reported that Scott Weekly, Lister's supposed CIA contact was not a CIA agent, but a right-wing mercenary who in the early 1980s, had unsuccessfully searched for U.S. prisoners of war in Laos with Bo Gritz, a former Lieutenant Colonel in the U.S. Special Forces. Photographs of Weekly from Gritz' memoir, *Called to Serve*, show Weekly in the jungle, weaving indigenous baskets with the phrase "Happy Reagan," apparently intended as gifts for local tribesmen.

According to press accounts in the early 1980s, Weekly, an explosive expert known as "Dr. Death," was an ex-Navy SEAL who won two bronze stars in Vietnam. While VeriSEAL, an organization that monitors SEAL impersonators, claims it has no records Weekly ever served in the outfit, he did attend the U.S. Naval Academy for three years.

Although he failed to graduate—his lawyer, Lynn Ball, told me the Navy booted him for having an affair with an admiral's daughter—one of his classmates was none other than Oliver North.

After "Dark Alliance," the L.A. Sheriff's Department questioned Lister and Weekly about their relationship to the CIA. Both Lister and Weekly acknowledged working together, but refused to elaborate. Lister told them their focus on the CIA was miscast. "You have to remember, there are thirty-two intelligence agencies out there; the CIA is just one of them," he said. Notes seized at Lister's home referred to Weekly as a Defense Intelligence Agency (DIA) "subcontractor" who had "worked in El Salvador for us." When investigators asked Weekly about the DIA, he refused to confirm or deny his relationship with the agency. "Let me put it this way, there is not one ounce of love lost between the DIA and me ," Weekly said. "It's a non-subject. As far as I'm concerned, I wouldn't piss on them if their face was on fire."

Weekly's animosity to the DIA goes unexplained in the Sheriff's report, but may involve his 1986 arrest for smuggling plastic explosives on a domestic flight from Oklahoma City to Las Vegas. Weekly spent fourteen months in prison for refusing to explain his actions, but the judge released him after determining that he had worked with the National Security Council's Defense Security Assistance Administration in a covert operation on federal government land in Nevada. Courtroom records from Weekly's trial in Oklahoma City show the explosives were used in a covert operation aimed at uniting the leaders of various Afghan rebel factions by providing them with lessons in explosives.

At Weekly's re-sentencing hearing, he and Gritz testified they carried out the operation in the Nevada desert with the permission of a U.S. Army colonel named Nestor Piño, who then worked with Oliver North's National Security Council, and that they were paid by Osman Kalderim, an employee of Stanford Technology, a private company established by two of North's Iran contra associates, Richard Secord and Albert Hakim, to help arm the contras. Letters of introduction Gritz published in his book show that within days of Lister's famous claim that Weekly worked for the CIA, Weekly and Gritz were meeting at the White House with National Security Council officials about the Nevada operation.

In 2001, French television journalist Paul Moreira interviewed ex-CIA agent Milton Bearden, who ran the agency's covert war in Afghanistan, about the mission. "The CIA could have been involved in that Bo Gritz thing," Bearden said. "I'm aware of that. I know about that. There's something like that. But it doesn't matter." Bearden's statement—five years after "Dark Alliance"—provided the first confirmation that Weekly was at times working for the CIA. And it directly contradicts the CIA's sworn declaration that it had no ties whatsoever to Weekly—an assertion that fueled the mainstream media's attacks on "Dark Alliance."

According to Moreira, Bearden made those comments shortly after the 9/11 terrorist attacks. "He was very surprised that I even knew about the existence of Bo Gritz," Moreira said. "In France, we call people like Gritz and Weekly *barbouzes* or 'beards' because they are a bunch of illegal guys who get used from time to time by government agencies when some action is not strictly legal. You cannot wage a war without these type of guys."

While behind bars, Weekly spoke with investigators for Mark Richards, an Iran contra prosecutor, about his participation in CIA activity in Central America. In a 1987 deposition obtained through the Freedom of Information Act from the National Archives, Richards said that Weekly "had post[ed] on tape that he's tied into CIA and [Eugene] Hasenfus," a reference to the hapless CIA-paid cargo handler who was shot down over Nicaragua in October 1986. Richards claimed that Weekly's telephone logs showed several calls to National Security Council officials, and that his investigators had found evidence that Weekly worked with Bo Gritz and a certain Tom "Lafrance" in San Diego.

When I tried to interview Weekly about Lister at his house in San Diego in early 1997, he didn't answer the door. After I peeked over his fence, he rushed outside, fists clenched, straight toward me. Upon learning I was a reporter—unarmed, except for a pad and pencil—he went back inside his house and refused to answer any questions.

However, Gritz told me that Weekly had likely met Lister at a San Diego automatic weapons dealership. Through the U.S. Bureau of Alcohol, Tobacco & Firearms, I discovered that there were only a handful of weapons dealers in San Diego licensed to sell fully automatic weapons, including Lafrance Specialties. The company's owner, Tim Lafrance—the "Tom" Lafrance mentioned in Richard's notes—works exclusively for government and military clients around the world.

In a series of interviews in 1996 and 1997, Lafrance stated that he had traveled to El Salvador with Lister and Weekly. He described Lister as a CIA asset and said his security company was a "favored vendor" used by the CIA "to do things it couldn't do." Lister "never received a paycheck from them," Lafrance said. "Very few people work directly for the agency. They deal with some pretty seedy bastards. Dealing with Lister, they probably got the clean end of the stick."

The ostensible reason for the trip was that Lister was negotiating to sell arms and security gear to the Salvadoran armed forces. Lafrance said he knew Lister's connections were good when he personally applied for a temporary import/export license from the State Department. "It came back in two days," he said. "Usually, it takes three months." While in El Salvador, Lafrance claimed, they stayed with the Atlcatl Battalion, the elite, U.S.-trained division that was the pride of the Salvadoran military during the civil war. "They gave us an opportunity to demonstrate our hardware."

But once they arrived in El Salvador, Lafrance continued, the real mission began: selling weapons to the contras. Government documents show that Lister didn't go unnoticed in El Salvador. A Freedom of Information Act request filed with the National Archives produced a May 12, 1987 FBI report concerning Lister's presence in the country. The report describes an interview that month with Federico Cruz, who approached an FBI office in Mobile, Alabama, seeking Lister's whereabouts. Cruz, who owned the Ramada Inn in San Salvador, claimed Lister traveled to El Salvador in 1982 and was "selling weapons to the contras." Cruz also told the FBI that members of the CIA team working with Hasenfus had stayed at his hotel, and that after his plane was shot down by the Sandinistas, somebody had cleaned out their rooms.

Further evidence of Lister's unusual "security" work in Central America was an October 1982 contract proposal that was seized in Lister's home four years later and released by the Sheriff's Department in 1996. Written in Spanish, the proposal was addressed to General Jose Guillermo Garcia, the Minister of Defense of El Salvador. Garcia, like Lister's other Salvadoran business contact, Roberto D'Aubuisson, had attended the U.S. Army School of the Americas, whose graduates read like a roster of Latin American CIA assets and human rights violators.

A member of the military junta that took over El Salvador in 1979, Garcia helped cover up the 1981 Atctatl battalion massacre of more than eight hundred villagers at the village of El Mozote. In 2002, he and Carlos Eugenio Vides Casanova, director of El Salvador's National Guard and Garcia's successor as Defense Minister, were fined $54.6 million by a Florida federal jury after being sued by several Salvadoran torture victims.

No two men were more powerful—or more feared—in El Salvador circa October 1982 than Garcia, the country's military leader, or D'Aubuisson, the reputed leader of the right-wing death squads. The pair jointly presided over a reign of terror responsible for hundreds of disappearances and murders each month. In particular, as Joan Didion wrote in her book *Salvador*, sixty-eight political murders occurred during the first half of that month.

"At the end of October 1982," Didion reported, "the

offices in the Hotel Camino Real in San Salvador of the Associated Press, United Press International Television News, NBC News, CBS News and ABC News were raided and searched by members of the El Salvador National Police carrying submachine guns; 15 leaders of legally recognized political and labor groups . . . were disappeared . . . the Salvadoran Ministry of Defense announced that eight of the 15 disappeared citizens were, in fact, in government custody; and the State Department announced that the Reagan administration believed that it had 'turned the corner' in its campaign for political stability in Central America."

In the midst of that carnage, Lister proposed to provide Garcia and other Salvadoran defense officials with security services, including the expertise of CIA-trained physical security experts and a manufacturer of "unique weapons." On the front page was the name of Lister's "technical director," a man named Richard E. Wilker. Lafrance recalled Wilker as the person who introduced him to Lister. "Wilker had heard about my stuff through the agency," Lafrance said. "He said he a had a friend who wanted to talk about a deal. I called to check, and [CIA headquarters in] Langley said [Wilker] was still working for the agency. So I started doing business with Lister and Wilker."

Although a quick check of California corporate records for Lister's company listed nobody by that name, Wilker worked for another Newport Beach company, Intersect, Inc. One of Intersect's principals, John Vandewerker, recalled that Lister and Wilker had a "touchy" time getting out of El Salvador. He denied that either man worked for the CIA, but nervously confirmed that he himself was a retired CIA agent.

The company's founder, Robert Barry Ashby, lives in northern Virginia. In a 1996 interview, Ashby recalled that Lister and Wilker had traveled to El Salvador together. He also denied that Lister or Wilker had any connection to the CIA, and said he knew this because he had retired from the agency in the mid-1970s. When I told Ashby that Lister was a convicted drug dealer who had claimed to work for the CIA, Ashby got nervous. "Has it ever occurred to you that some people might not be happy about what you're writing about?" he said.

The fact that Lister—just a "con artist" in the words of the *LA Times*—was on speaking terms with retired CIA agents is weird, to say the least. But Lister had even more unusual friends. While researching "Dark Alliance," Webb had discovered that Lister apparently was meeting with a retired CIA covert operations chief. Lister's employee, Christopher Moore, who told Webb he met face to face with D'Aubuisson, said that before leaving for El Salvador, Lister met frequently with an executive at an Orange County construction company—a man whom Lister claimed was an ex-CIA official.

"I can't remember his name, but Ron was always running off to meetings with him, supposedly," Moore told Webb. "Ron said the guy was the former deputy director of operations or something, real high up there. All I know is that this supposed contact of his was working at the Fluor Corp., because I had to call Ron out there a couple of times." As Lister and Moore prepared to travel to the war-wracked country, Lister told Moore that they'd be "protected" on the trip.

In the raid on Lister's house, deputies found a handwritten list of his business contacts. Next to Scott Weekly and Roberto D'Aubuisson was the name Bill Nelson. When Sheriff's detectives interviewed Lister about Nelson in 1996, he claimed Nelson was a vice president for security at Fluor Corp. That would be a distinct understatement. In the early 1990s, David Corn of the *Nation* magazine had interviewed William E. Nelson for his book, *Blond Ghost*, a biography of CIA agent Ted Shackley. Nelson knew Shackley because before he joined Fluor Corp., Nelson was the CIA's deputy director of operations.

Nelson died of natural causes in 1995, so there was no way to ask him why his name was in Lister's notes. It wasn't until six years after Webb published "Dark Alliance" that I received heavily censored FBI records about Lister and Nelson in response to a 1997 Freedom of Information Act request. The records confirmed that Lister and Nelson had an eight years business relationship. The exact nature of that relationship remains unclear, because the FBI refuses to release uncensored copies, arguing that to do so would jeopardize U.S. national security.

But what is clear from the heavily redacted records is that, in 1985—while Lister was still laundering drug money to the contras and providing weapons to Blandon—the FBI began investigating one of his international arms deals. The investigation somehow led to Nelson, who told the FBI he had recently stopped doing business with Lister after the latter got in trouble with the FBI. Nelson admitted calling other retired CIA agents on Lister's behalf, but told Lister "nobody at the CIA can help you until you clear yourself with the FBI."

Nelson also admitted that Lister had sought his advice before testifying before a grand jury. "He [Lister] then told of his meeting with the FBI and that he had been subpoenaed before the grand jury in San Francisco," the FBI memo states. "He told Nelson he was terrified. Nelson said go . . . [Lister] admitted being stupid and that he had done a dumb thing. Nelson said [Lister] left and then called back after his grand-jury appearance and said he did really well."

During his FBI interrogation, Nelson claimed Lister had also applied for a job with Fluor. "He was never offered a job," the memo states. The FBI censored the next sentence, but the memo continues, "Nelson thought Fluor might be able to use his [Lister's] company. Nelson said [Lister] started traveling overseas, Lebanon and Central America, and he always had some scheme that never materialized."

In a late 1996 interview, Vandewerker told me Lister had also helped him apply for a job at Fluor. "For a while, I tried to get a job at Fluor when I stopped working, and I know Rich [Wilker] was trying to sell something to Fluor," he said.

The fact that Nelson seemed to be a source of potential employment for ex-CIA agents like Vandewerker, not to mention a "con artist" like Lister, is ironic, given that one of Nelson's final acts at the CIA was to recommend the agency terminate full-time jobs for agents who were "marginal" performers. "We owe these people a lot," Nelson wrote then-CIA director George Bush in a 1976 memo. "But not a lifetime job."

Although Lister escaped arrest during the 1986 raid on

his Mission Viejo house, his coke dealing quickly caught up with him. Two years later, he tried to sell two kilos of cocaine to a prostitute he met at a Newport Beach boat party. The woman turned out to be a Costa Mesa police informant, and Lister ended up behind bars for the first time since he began working with Blandon and Meneses six years earlier. Two kilos was enough to land Lister in prison for years; instead he walked out of jail after only two days.

Lister had signed a deal with the Orange County district attorney's office. After he told police about "boatloads" of marijuana off the coast of California ready for "offloading," prosecutors let him go. But his new career as an informant was short-lived. The following year, San Diego police arrested Lister again, this time in connection with a local cocaine distribution ring.

Lister got out on bail, and got a job working with his friend Scott Weekly in San Diego. But Lister quickly came to the DEA's attention during their investigation of Jose Urda, Jr., a Chula Vista accountant who was laundering money for the Colombian coke cartels. Urda told undercover DEA agents posing as Colombian drug merchants that his colleague, a San Diego car dealer, had met Lister in San Diego's Metropolitan Correctional Center. After Urda requested his assistance, Lister agreed to help Urda launder $30,000 per day for his Colombian clients.

During their investigation, undercover DEA agents posing as Colombian traffickers infiltrated a meeting with Lister in Urda's living room. Also present were a pair of actual Colombian dealers who wanted $500,000 back from Lister, who said he couldn't return the cash because he had laundered it with the CIA's help and didn't want to arouse the bank's suspicion. In fact, Lister bragged, he "used to transport multi-hundred kilos of cocaine from Cali, Colombia, to the U.S." with the CIA's help.

The Colombians weren't impressed. The DEA agents in the room overheard one of them remark in Spanish that Lister was a "dead man." Without blowing their cover, one of the agents told Lister he'd better find the money. According to a DEA report, "Lister replied that he had nothing to fear since he worked for the CIA." The Colombians meant business, and Lister came close to regretting his bluster. On June 19, 1991, federal agents at an immigration checkpoint near San Diego nabbed a four-member cartel hit team that had been dispatched to kill Lister.

That year, a jury convicted Lister on drug-trafficking charges; he was sentenced to ninety-seven months in prison and sixty months of probation. Lister appealed, asserting that while an informant, he had testified before two federal grand juries about a "major Central American cartel" and his "activities in Central America concerning certain key figures from Nicaragua alleged to have been involved in the Iran contra scandal."

In establishing grounds for a softer sentence, Lister told the court he had certainly run drugs, but he had also cooperated with the government. He claimed he gave prosecutors thousands of pages of documents and notes regarding his work for the CIA "from 1982 to 1986 and beyond, and I did it in detail, location, activity," he said. "I gave them physical evidence, phone bills, travel tickets, everything possible back from those days—which most people don't keep, but I do keep good records—to assist them in this investigation. They were excited about it."

Lister got out of prison shortly after "Dark Alliance" appeared, and has rebuffed all efforts to be interviewed. While much mystery surrounds—and most likely always will surround—the exact nature of his ties to the CIA, what is certain is that he was more than simply a "con artist," as asserted by the *LA Times*. Lister's business deals with powerful Salvadoran officials, his role in supplying the contras with arms, his relationship to retired CIA officials, and his ties to Blandon and Meneses all suggest that the "Dark Alliance" drug ring had closer ties to the CIA then even Webb could have known.

SEVERAL MONTHS AFTER the CIA and Justice Department released their initial reports on "Dark Alliance," the CIA's Inspector General released a second volume, a more wide-ranging probe of contra drug trafficking and an accounting of what the agency did—or as more often proved the case—didn't do about it. The report's chief admission: between 1982 and 1995, the CIA did not report drug dealing by its assets, under an agreement signed between the agency and the Justice Department. But the CIA got a jump-start on that policy when it came to the Nicaraguan contras. The agency knew as early as 1981 that one element of the contras "had decided to engage in drug trafficking to the United States to raise funds for its activities."

The specific group in question was the 15th of September Legion, which at the time was led by Enrique Bermudez,

the contra commander who met with Blandon and Meneses in Honduras and allegedly told them that "the ends justify the means" when it came to raising cash. Without
mentioning Blandon or Meneses, the CIA report acknowledged that the agency knew that supporters of Bermudez
were funding contra operations with drug money, and the
CIA didn't lift a finger to stop it.

The CIA also admitted that Ivan Gomez, the CIA agent
Carlos Cabezas told Webb had supervised Meneses' drug
pipeline, was actually a pseudonym used by a CIA agent in
Costa Rica. But the CIA claimed it could find no evidence
that Gomez, who later left the agency because of his ties to
drug traffickers, had ever met with Cabezas.

To its credit, the *New York Times* gave the CIA report
front-page treatment. Walter Pincus of the *Washington Post*
also wrote about the agency's stunning admission, although
not on the front page. He concluded, "the report contradicts
previous CIA claims that it had little information about
drug running and the contras." But failing to mention that
the CIA specifically suspected Bermudez and his supporters of drug trafficking, Pincus added that the report "does
not lend any new support to charges of an alliance among
the CIA, contra fund-raisers and dealers who introduced
crack-cocaine in the 1980s in South Central Los Angeles."

"Pincus writes off twelve years of official lies by the CIA
as mere contradiction," Webb argued in a letter to the
editor of the *Post*. While the report did contradict previous
CIA statements about the contras and drugs, Webb added
that it also contradicted most of what the *Post* had reported
about the issue for the past two decades. "Ordinary citizens

can be jailed for such lawless conduct," Webb wrote. "That your paper continues to minimize criminal behavior when the CIA engages in it is most peculiar."

The *LA Times* didn't even bother writing a story about the second CIA Inspector General report. Doyle McManus acknowledges this was a major failure by his newspaper. "The critics are correct that the *LA Times* did not give enough attention to the findings in the CIA's Inspector General's report about the agency's failure to report information about drug dealing to law enforcement agencies," McManus says. "We dropped the ball on that story."

Former Kerry Committee prosecutor Jack Blum believes the *LA Times* and other newspapers intentionally downplayed the second CIA report because it vindicated the Kerry Committee investigation, which they had largely ignored at the time. It reminded Blum of the media's tendency to put stories about Kerry's investigation in the Saturday edition, deep inside the paper—or on "Saturday below the fold," as he said at the time. "I think they were terribly embarrassed when the reports came out," Blum says. "Those reports vindicated Gary Webb and our committee, so they buried it. The coverage was not spectacular. The adage of 'Saturday below the fold' was still in vogue."

The National Security Archives' Peter Kornbluh doesn't think the CIA's Inspector General report vindicated "Dark Alliance." Although the uproar over Webb's story finally forced the CIA to come clean about its protection of contra drug traffickers, most of the activities in the report had nothing to do with the people in Webb's story. "I can't say it's a vindication," he says. "It was good that his story forced those reports to come out, but part of what made that happen was based on misleading information."

David Corn of the *Nation* magazine says the CIA report only "partially" vindicated Webb. "It didn't vindicate his story," he says. "It vindicated his interest in the subject and his belief that this was important and that something terribly rotten had happened." Nonetheless, Corn feels that the reports contained "tremendous admissions" of wrongdoing by the CIA. "While Nancy Reagan was saying 'Just say No,' the CIA was saying, 'Just don't look,' " he says.

Corn is still amazed that the fact that the CIA finally admitted it had worked with and protected from prosecution Nicaraguan contra drug traffickers—and then lied about it for years—wasn't a major scandal. "Here you have the CIA acknowledging they were working with people suspected of drug dealing and it got nary a peep," he says. "I think in some ways that's journalistic neglect—criminal neglect. In what definition of news is it not a front-page story that the CIA was working with drug dealers?"

Exile ELEVEN

WEBB'S SEPARATION FROM his family while working in Cupertino—and his sudden exit from journalism shortly thereafter—precipitated a long slide into depression that would last the rest of his life. But at first, the experience brought him closer to his wife than he had been in years. Sue stood faithfully by her husband, and encouraged him to write a book that would allow him to do what his editors had refused to allow him to accomplish: publish everything he'd unearthed about the CIA, the contras, and drugs.

In the year that had passed since "Dark Alliance" had been appeared, however, the major publishing houses were no longer interested. Webb could scarcely find an editor willing to read his book proposal. After more than twenty rejections, he signed a deal with Seven Stories Press, an independent publisher that specializes in progressive books, including its annual "Project Censored" compendium of investigative stories overlooked by the mainstream media each year.

Dan Simon, publisher of Seven Stories Press, says the "Dark Alliance" controversy killed Webb's prospects overnight. "The minute those front page stories ran basically trashing this guy nobody would touch him," Simon says. "Nobody wanted anything to do with Gary Webb." Unlike Webb's editors at the *Mercury News*, who had mercilessly hacked away his series to fit it in the paper, Simon read Webb's lengthy first draft, and encouraged him to write even more. "I told him this was his opportunity to put everything in there," he says. "We used to talk at night from 8 to 11 PM, after he got home from work and we had a great time. It was a lot of fun. He was like a pig in mud."

Simon saw Webb as a heroic journalist who had been castigated for writing a story that was ultimately vindicated by the CIA itself. Between the book's 1998 hardcover release and its publication the next year as a paperback, the CIA had released its Inspector General report revealing that the agency had lied for years about its protection of Nicaraguan contra drug traffickers. "I can't tell you how intensely excited he was about this," Simon says. "The lesson to him was not only did everything he had said turn out to be completely vindicated by those reports, but it was clear to him he had actually understated the story. To the end of his days, Gary felt that very clearly the story was much bigger than he had realized."

Webb wrote the book mostly at night and on the weekends. Shortly after leaving the *Mercury News*, he landed a job as a well-paid investigator for the California Joint Legislative Audit Committee. The position not only matched his previous salary and allowed him to continue to work in Sacramento, but was perfectly suited to his skills: Webb would spend the next several years uncovering government corruption and bureaucratic ineptitude in state government.

While writing his book, Sue says, her husband became distant. With three kids running around the house, and her husband writing all day, Sue found herself increasingly frustrated at the burden that came with trying to be a supportive wife. With even more determination than he'd put into his previous work, Webb had thrown himself into his new project. He was determined not to leave out anything, no matter how remotely significant, that would help clear his name.

All the long hours he spent at the computer, reliving the excruciating experience he'd just undergone at the *Mercury News*, came with a certain emotional toll, however. Webb didn't have any new discoveries to share at the dinner table. More often than not, he was still writing at dinnertime. Meanwhile, Webb had grown increasingly troubled, not paranoid exactly, but uncharacteristically concerned about his family's security. He kept a gun stashed in his bedroom. The telephone would sometimes ring, but nobody was there. In the middle of a conversation, Sue would sometimes hear clicks on the line.

One evening, Sue noticed that her husband seemed especially quiet. When she asked him what was wrong, he told her that he'd met with a source that had said something that bothered him. "He was told that he'd be killed one day," she says. The man had darkly suggested that it wouldn't happen anytime soon, perhaps not until five or ten years in the future, and it wouldn't be anything obvious. As an example, the man explained, one day Webb might be driving down a steep slope in the mountains and his brakes would fail. "I was pretty upset about it," Sue says. "But Gary told me, 'Oh, you can't go around worrying about that kind of thing. It might happen, it might not, but I'm not going to go through my life worrying about it and looking over my shoulder all the time.'"

Dark Alliance: The CIA, The Contras, and The Crack Cocaine Explosion received mixed reviews in the mainstream press, but even critics acknowledged it was a much more nuanced and convincing, if vastly more complicated, work of journalism than his heavily-edited *Mercury News* series. *Washington Post* media critic Howard Kurtz, who had last written about Webb a year earlier when he was transferred to Cupertino—"the *Mercury News* has apparently had enough of reporter Gary Webb"—continued to heap scorn. " 'Dark Alliance' is back," he wrote ominously, adding that Webb had to settle for "a small [publishing] house" after receiving a "torrent of rejections."

The book received no television coverage, with the exception of C-SPAN, which invited Webb to answer phone calls from viewers, most of whom had little to say about *Dark Alliance*, and a lot to say about whatever they had read in the newspaper that morning. When one caller asked Webb what he thought of a story talking about a then-unknown Saudi dissident named Osama bin Laden, who had just declared war on the United States, Webb said it appeared bin Laden was angry because the U.S. had put troops on Saudi soil during the Persian Gulf war. "It sounds like just another example of our policies coming back to haunt us," he said.

The *Mercury News* didn't bother to review the book, the *New York Times* concluded that Webb still hadn't done enough to verify his allegations with CIA insiders, while the *LA Times* dismissed it as "densely researched, passionately argued, [and] acronym-laden." The *Baltimore Sun* gave a much more favorable review, and even the *Washington Post* grudgingly congratulated Webb for forcing the CIA to shed light on its "sleazy past."

"That's as close to an apology as Webb ever received" from the papers that had helped end his career, says publisher Dan Simon. But the accolades Webb received for his book from liberal fans didn't provide him with much solace. "Gary went from being a hero of the establishment to being vilified by that club to being a hero of the American left," he says. "Getting awards didn't matter to Gary. He appreciated it but it didn't comfort him at all, because they weren't his people."

Mixed reviews didn't keep people from buying the book. According to publisher Dan Simon, *Dark Alliance* wasn't a best seller, but enjoyed strong sales—which continue today, eight years later—thanks to Webb's notoriety. On his book tour, crowds filled bookstores from San Francisco and Los Angeles to New York and Washington, D.C., as Webb traveled around the country giving speeches and signing autographs. With his newfound status as an exiled reporter, progressive audiences hailed

Webb as a hero. Not all audiences were pleased with what he had to say, however. At the Midnight Special bookstore in Santa Monica, some members in the audience were shocked when Webb began his speech by explaining that he never believed the CIA had conspired to flood America's inner cities with crack cocaine.

One serious-looking African-American woman interrupted his speech to announce that Webb had his facts wrong. "The police invented crack," she said, her arms folded defiantly. "No, they didn't," Webb responded, looking down at his notes, struggling to regain his stream of thought. "What happened was this drug ring, which the CIA has now admitted it protected, arrived in South-Central at a particularly bad time, in 1982," he said. "It hooked up with the gangs right when people in South-Central were learning how to turn powder cocaine into crack."

"Don't try to tell us that!" the woman responded, her voice rising in frustration. "The police invented that drug." She then claimed that undercover police informants had broken into her house and fed her intravenous drugs "so they can turn me into another statistic."

Like former CIA Director John Deutch, who defended his agency to a similarly irate crowd in South Central shortly after Webb's story appeared, Webb did his best to push through with his speech. But the more he talked, the angrier people got. It wasn't necessarily that anyone disagreed with what Webb was saying. It was more the fact that many in the audience hadn't arrived to hear Webb talk about the CIA, but to bury the spy agency with their own words.

"I think we all appreciate what you've done, but we just

want you to tell the whole truth about the CIA," one of the audience's white members helpfully explained, stopping Webb's speech to launch into a diatribe about the agency's genocidal plot to wipe out black America. The audience began screaming and cheering in unison—not at the man's remark, but because U.S. Congresswoman Maxine Waters had arrived just in time for the end of Webb's speech. Waters strode straight up to the podium and embraced Webb. In a single hug, the rage of decades of distrust between African Americans and the CIA, which seemed ready to devour even Webb just moments earlier, mercifully subsided.

BACK IN CALIFORNIA, Sue was paying the telephone bill one afternoon when she noticed an expensive long-distance call that Webb had made late one night from his hotel room on the East Coast to someone in the Bay Area. The call had lasted for more than an hour. When Webb returned, Sue confronted him about the mysterious phone call, and he admitted he was having an affair with a woman—a former source he had met while researching "Dark Alliance." "I wasn't sure what to do," Sue says. "We had three kids and I didn't ever want to get a divorce."

Sue didn't kick her husband out of the house. When Webb offered to break off the relationship, she suggested they try couple's counseling. Sitting in a therapist's office, Webb decided to come clean. He told Sue that the affair wasn't his first. His first fling had been while he still worked for the *Cleveland Plain Dealer*. It had happened just as Webb received an offer to move to California and work at the *Mercury News*; the woman had called him at home. It terrified him so much he decided to move to California.

In therapy, Webb confessed that the phone call played a critical role in his decision to leave the *Plain Dealer*. "That's why we moved here," Sue says. "He didn't want to have another affair. But when we moved to California, he made a vow that he would change. And he did change. I know he was faithful after we moved. It was only after he wrote his book when everything fell apart."

According to Sue, it wasn't the first time her husband had raised the subject of infidelity. Two decades earlier, when Webb was still at the *Kentucky Post*, he had told Sue that he was disturbed by a friendship he was having with another woman. He thought it might go somewhere, he said. He was meeting her for lunch regularly, talking to her on the phone almost every day. Webb's parents had recently divorced because of his father's infidelity, and Webb had promised himself he'd never cheat on his wife. "Gary said, 'I am telling you this because it's scaring me,' Sue recalls. "That devastated me. And in therapy, Gary said that was why he never told me about the other affairs, because he saw the effect it had on me."

Therapy failed to hold the marriage together. One weekday morning in the spring of 1999, after a half year of therapy sessions, just after the kids had left for school, Sue became suspicious that her husband was having another affair. It happened halfway through a casual conversation, when Webb mentioned the name of a woman he knew at work. Sue grabbed the opportunity and demanded to know if he was sleeping with the woman. Webb knew he'd been caught and didn't deny it.

Sue was speechless. She had remained by her husband's side during the toughest years of his career, taking care of the children while he was away from home chasing after his big story, and again after his own newspaper had exiled him to Cupertino. The months he spent writing his book hadn't been easy, either. "He was working all the time, but telling me that pretty soon, it was all going to be over, and everything was going to be fine again. I was looking forward to that, and then I find out he was having an affair, and I was furious."

The couple sat on the couch in their living room waiting for their kids to get back from school so they could tell them their father was leaving that night. Webb didn't look back. He moved into an apartment, and according to his high school friend Greg Wolf, quickly began dating a series of women. None of the relationships lasted very long. Webb had also begun taking anti-depressant medication and was smoking pot on a daily basis.

By then, Webb had lost interest in his job at the California State Legislature. It had started off well enough. His first assignment, for the legislature's joint audit committee, was to investigate racial profiling by the California Highway Patrol (CHP). Working from reports on traffic stops and interviews with dozens of officers, he turned in a report showing that minority drivers were far more likely than whites to be pulled over, while the overwhelming majority of searches for drugs and weapons turned up nothing.

Webb's findings raced serious questions about the justification used to make such stops. CHP records showed that once they stopped vehicles on the freeway, officers could demand to search vehicles for drugs based on the presence of anything from fast food wrappers to out-of-state license plates. Webb also uncovered evidence that certain CHP officers were providing seminars on racial profiling to patrolmen throughout the state.

But according to Webb's colleague, Tom Dresslar, now a spokesman for California Attorney General Bill Lockyer, Antonio Villaraigosa, then speaker of the California Assembly and later mayor of Los Angeles, prevented the report from being released. "The whole thing was true," Dresslar says. "But this report was embarrassing to the CHP, so Villaraigosa made up some excuse about it not being ready for publication and killed it."

Mike Madigan, a private investigator in Orange County who also runs an online journal about police corruption, www.twistedbadge.com, met Webb at a 1998 journalism conference and kept in touch with him over the years, trying to convince him to become a private investigator. While Webb was working on CHP report, Madigan had been hired by a lawyer to conduct surveillance on CHP officers in Needles, California, a desert town on Interstate 40 halfway between Los Angeles and Las Vegas. Madigan and his partner witnessed highway patrolmen armed with binoculars as they routinely pulled over minorities suspected of transporting drugs.

"We used to watch these officers looking for cars that had deodorizers, or that looked like they were carrying a heavy load, or that had a female with a male of a different ethnic background," Madigan says. "They would pull them over for any reason and search the cars." Madigan couldn't wait for Webb to release his report. "It was going to tell the truth about what was going on," he says. "The CHP was sanctioning a program that was educating its officers on how to violate the rights of minorities without getting caught. The CHP expected Gary to write the report they way they saw things, but he didn't. As soon as he filed that report, they took his name off his door."

On April 1, 1999, Webb published the results of his findings in a lengthy article for *Esquire* magazine entitled "DWB," a slang term among minority motorists that stands for "Driving While Black." A year earlier, *Esquire* had published "The Pariah," a haunting feature story about the "Dark Alliance" controversy by author Charles Bowden. After the CHP fiasco, Webb was transferred to the Office of Majority Services, where his talents were wasted. "That's where they put the hacks who really have nothing to contribute except working on political campaigns," Dresslar says. "They gave him all these bullshit political hack jobs, and he didn't want to do them. I guess his attendance record wasn't good."

Anita Webb, who then lived in Los Alamitos, recalled her son calling her from Long Beach, where he had been sent to canvas on behalf of a local Democratic candidate. "He was furious about that," she says. "He called me up and says, 'I'm staying her at this hotel with this other guy and I have to share a room." Anita invited her son to stay at her condominium until he returned to Sacramento. "He was very morose at the time," she says. "He was upset because he had to do this legwork for the Democratic Party. And you couldn't talk to him about it. He didn't want to elaborate. Gary was just closing himself off."

Ian Webb says his father's occasional bouts of depression never seemed chronic until he worked at the legislature. "It wasn't anything he really wanted to do," he says. "Sometimes I'd be talking to him on the phone and he sounded just melancholy. He'd talk in this monotone voice. And he'd never really go into work because they didn't give him anything to do. That's when he really got into motorcycles, because he would always have a lot of free time."

Ian and his father often rode together. He says the times he spent riding with his dad were the happiest experiences they had shared since he was in junior high school, when Webb coached Ian's hockey team. "We'd ride into the mountains and make a day trip out of it," he says. "We'd find a place to eat. It was a great way to relieve stress." Ian noticed that, over time, his father's reflexes weren't quite as good, a possible effect of taking anti-depressants. In the winter, when the weather got too cold to ride, Webb would typically be in a sour mood. "I remember talking to him on the phone when there had been a long period of overcast days," Ian says. "I said, 'This really sucks.' And he said, 'Depressing is what it is.'"

When Greg Wolf's mother died in 2000, Webb flew back to Indianapolis to attend the funeral. In the four years that had passed since Wolf last saw him on the eve of "Dark Alliance," his friend had changed. Webb no longer seemed to have a sense of humor. "I don't know if the fame got to him or what the hell happened," Wolf says. "He just didn't seem very empathetic. He just seemed lost."

Webb's divorce didn't become final until September 2000. The day the paperwork cleared, Webb crashed his motorcycle when a young woman turned in front of him. Webb went flying into the street, but escaped with only minor injuries. He continued to date various women, but after a series of breakups, managed to reconcile with his ex-wife. The two began dating again. They got together on weekends to have dinner or see a movie, but kept the relationship secret from the kids to keep them from getting confused. Then Webb surprised Sue with two roundtrip tickets to Mexico. A photograph taken on their vacation reveals a smiling, suntanned couple apparently very much in love.

"It was beautiful," Sue says. "That was one of the best vacations we ever had." But the moment they arrived back in Sacramento, they were transported back to the reality of their divorce. Sue was still hurt by her husband's infidelity. Although he professed his love for her, he expected her unconditional trust, and she wasn't ready to give it. Sue suggested they take a break from each other and see what happened. "He said, 'Okay, if that's what you want to do,'" Sue says.

When Sue told her husband she wanted a break, that's exactly what she meant—not that they'd never get back together, but that they take some time to figure out if they were truly ready to revive their marriage. Her answer came a few months later, when she learned that Webb had been involved in another motorcycle accident. While riding in the mountains with some friends near Reno, Nevada, he had skidded on loose gravel and lost control.

It was a hard fall that cracked Webb's helmet. But he

brushed himself off, got back on his bike, and rode on. On the ride back to California, however he passed out and went off the road into a meadow. As his bike sputtered nearby, Webb dangled from a barbed wire fence, unconscious and bleeding from a ruptured spleen from his earlier accident. He had had to be airlifted to a hospital. When Sue offered to go visit him, he acted nervous, telling her not to bother; it was too long a drive. She found out a few weeks later that he had already started dating a reporter he'd gotten to know at work.

According to Sue and her son Ian, Webb's new girlfriend was a positive influence on his life. He seemed dedicated to her, and despite years of growing depression, appeared happy again. They moved in together, and Webb began showing more interest in his job. By now, Webb had been transferred back to the joint legislative audit committee to work with Dresslar, probing the state's energy crisis. The two also investigated charges that the Oracle Corporation had received a no-bid contract award worth $95 million from former California Governor Gray Davis.

"He worked his ass off," Dresslar says. The day he and Webb got the assignment, they stayed in the office until 4 AM doing research. Later, they interviewed all the witnesses to the awarding of the contract, wrote up a timeline, and provided the committee with a report that led to several Davis administration officials losing their jobs. "He was happy," Dresslar says. "The job utilized the talents he had. You could tell he loved the work. It was like being a reporter, but you didn't have to hand your stuff off to an editor. We had a blast."

In late 2002 however, Dresslar accepted a job with California Attorney General Lockyer's office when he came to the conclusion that the committee's new leadership wasn't serious about investigating corruption. Webb kept his job, but went back to doing pointless grunt work for Democratic candidates at the Office of Majority Services. Occasionally, Dresslar would invite Webb out to grab a beer, but Webb always had an excuse not to go. Although Webb was still living under the same roof with his girlfriend, they were no longer dating, and Webb's depression deepened to despair. She told Sue that simply being in the same room with him was too much for her to bear.

Withdrawal TWELVE

DESPITE HIS SEEMING downward spiral, Webb enjoyed happier moments. In January 2003, he attended a journalism conference on the Isla de Mujeres, an island resort off the coast of Cancun, Mexico, which had been organized by Al Giordano, an expatriate American reporter. Giordano's conference brought together young journalists from around Latin America interested in covering the war on drugs. (Giordano initially agreed to an interview, but only in writing; he failed to respond to subsequent emails.) Webb, who gave speeches about investigative reporting at the conference, was given a hero's welcome, says Jeremy Bigwood, a freelance photographer who attended the conference and helped Webb coach the younger journalists on accessing government records.

"He was known as the 'Marlboro Man' because he smoked Marlboro Reds and looked like the Marlboro man in the poster," Bigwood recalls. "Al was the first to call him that and it really took off." Despite the presence of a large contingent of beautiful young South American female reporters who fawned over him, Webb behaved himself well, Bigwood says. "Al had gotten a lot more women than men at this conference, but I think Gary saw that people were looking up to him and he gave a really good impression. Everyone really liked him."

Also at the conference was Adam Saytanides, a producer with National Public Radio's Latino USA. Saytanides met Webb at the airport and rode to the conference with him, and quickly realized that Webb was going to be the highlight of the conference. "Gary was a fucking Pulitzer-prize winner and he couldn't get a job in journalism." he says. "Gary was kind of a stud, because he was an example of that crash and burn mentality: publishing these stories and going out in a blaze of glory."

One of Webb's fellow lecturers was Annie Nocenti, a screenplay writer from New York City who had edited several magazines, including *Lies of Our Times*, *Scenario*, and *Prison Life*. Nocenti says she was immediately attracted to Webb. "He was an all-American boy, chivalrous, respectful, rugged, adventurous," she says. Webb rented a motorcycle, and the pair tore off to the beach, skipping an entire day of panel discussions to lie in the sun, a romantic interlude that quickly turned into a brief love affair.

To Nocenti, Webb didn't seem depressed in the least. "He was happy," she says. Although Webb had by then pulled away from many of his closest friends, Nocenti says he opened up with her about his life. He told her that he hated his job at the state legislature because it involved little more than showing up for work and trying to seem interested in meaningless, tedious assignments. Webb also talked about his experience at the *Mercury News*, and how his series was attacked for alleging that the CIA had dumped crack in the inner city—something he emphatically denied he had ever written.

"For some reason, he didn't seem particularly angry about it," she adds. Nocenti says they kept in touch by telephone after the conference ended, but didn't remain romantically involved. Webb told her he was still in love with his ex-girlfriend, but she didn't want to commit, so he was moving out of the house he shared with her and buying a fixer-upper. A few months after the conference, Webb flew to New York for an award that he shared for writing a chapter about "Dark Alliance" for *Into the Buzzsaw*, a book of essays by reporters who had been ousted from journalism after writing controversial stories.

While in New York City, Webb stayed with Nocenti, who introduced him to her friends, all of who were fans of his work. A TV producer Nocenti knew told Webb he wanted to put "Dark Alliance" on the screen. At one point, Webb expressed an interest in moving to New York, but said he couldn't leave California because he wanted to remain close to his children. When Nocenti got a job as the editor of *High Times* magazine a few months later, Webb told her he wanted to write a Hunter S. Thompson-style story about racing motorcycles against kids half his age. She loved the idea, but he never followed through.

On the phone, Webb seemed increasingly trapped in his own obsession over his ex-girlfriend. "He was in daily contact with a powerful unrequited love situation," Nocenti says. Nocenti tried to convince him to move on with his life, to forget about her. "But he thought she was so perfect," she says. "He said he'd only had two soul mates in his entire life, his ex-wife and this girl."

IF WEBB HAD still been married, February 10, 2004, would have been his twenty-fifth wedding anniversary. He marked the occasion in an email he sent Sue at 8:15 that morning.

"It might seem odd to commemorate the 25th anniversary of a marriage that no longer exists, but I've never been one to do the normal thing," Webb wrote. "Irrespective of everything else . . . today isn't a completely meaningless event in the history of our lives. Anyway, I just wanted you to know that I was thinking about you, my child bride, and that day a quarter century ago . . . it makes me sad and makes me smile at the same time."

Webb found out less than two hours later that this day would be a more meaningful one than he could have imagined. That morning, he was laid off, a casualty of the Democrats having lost control of the California Legislature and a concomitant change in leadership at the Office of Majority Services. His previous poor attendance record didn't help. After she heard the news, Sue emailed her ex-husband at 10 PM, telling him she wished it could have been a more "peaceful" day for him.

At 1 AM the next morning, Webb wrote back, the optimism

of his previous message replaced with stark fatalism. "I almost hate to wake up in the morning to see what shit the day will bring," he said. The only bright news, he added, was that he received a "couple of encouraging emails" from Gary Clark, his old friend from the *Plain Dealer*, who was now managing editor of the *Denver Post*. "I figure I can hold out for a couple of months," Webb wrote. "Then after that . . . who knows? You were right about moving out here. Except for Christine being born, I can't think of anything good that's come from living out here. The rest of it has been shit and heartbreak. Sorry."

In a recent interview, Clark says Webb had contacted him shortly before he lost his job, wanting to know if there was any possibility of getting a job at the *Denver Post*. Clark told Webb he might be in luck—the paper was interested in hiring an investigative reporter. Clark thought Webb would be perfect for the job. "Gary was probably one of the best reporters I ever met," he says. "He had this internal drive to go find the truth. He did that through ferreting out documents and evidence. Some people thought he was difficult to work with, but I didn't. He needed a strong editor though, that's for sure."

Before Clark could hire Webb, however, the paper had to hire an editor to oversee investigative coverage. "That search took a little longer than we expected," he says. Clark says he knew all about the controversy over "Dark Alliance," and it didn't particularly trouble him. "Gary had a story there," he says. "There were people on the CIA payroll engaged in deals that involved bringing cocaine to California, and that's what Gary's story was about." The story's lead was marred by a certain degree of hyperbole, but Clark says he's certain this was a result of bad editing. "Nobody above Gary's editor looked at that story before it ran," he says. "How it was presented was the issue."

Webb also contacted his friend Mike Madigan, the private investigator in Orange County he had met years earlier at a journalism conference. Madigan offered to help Webb obtain his private investigator's license and get him started in the field. But when Webb applied for his license, Madigan says, the California Department of Consumer Affairs refused to give Webb credit for his two decades of reporting experience. Noting that Webb hadn't finished college, the state told him he'd have to get his degree first. Webb gave up. "Gary told me he just couldn't start from scratch," Madigan says.

Webb's daughter Christine helped him send out more than fifty resumes to daily newspapers across the country. He didn't receive a single request for an interview. The only paper that seemed interested in hiring him was a local alternative newsweekly, the *Sacramento News & Review*. The paper's editor, Tom Walsh, had previously met Webb and told him if he was ever interested in writing for the paper to call him. When Webb contacted him in August 2004, Walsh happened to have an open position for a staff writer and suggested Webb drop by for an interview.

Despite Webb's impressive resume, which included twenty years of reporting experience and a Pulitzer prize, he wasn't Walsh's first choice. Now editor of the *SF Weekly*, Walsh says his leading candidate had a proven record in alternative journalism. Walsh, meanwhile, was concerned that Webb was overqualified for the job. He was looking for someone who would stick around, and figured Webb would likely use the job as a springboard to find employment at a larger paper. "Quite frankly, I had thoughts in the back of my mind about whether he would fit in," Walsh adds. "But the first person I offered the job declined, and I think at the time Gary said he could start immediately."

The only hitch was that Walsh couldn't offer Webb a salary that came close to matching the paycheck Webb had been receiving while an employee of the State of California. But Webb was desperate for work and jumped at the opportunity. Unlike the rest of the paper's small staff, however, most of whom were still fresh out of college, Webb was almost fifty years old. He made no effort to fit in with his fellow reporters.

"He would show up to our Monday meetings and have straightforward comments about what was interesting and what was not," Walsh says. "That was part of the value he brought." But whenever the staff got together to have beers, Webb declined. "He told me specifically he didn't drink," Walsh says. "He wasn't a party person. He didn't socialize. He would come in to do writing and do phone calls, but would also work at home."

Webb's first feature story for the paper, "The Killing Game," appeared in October 2004. It detailed the military's growing interest in violent video games, something Webb discovered by playing on the computer with his teenage son, Eric. According to Walsh, the story displayed all the talents that made Webb such a masterful reporter. "It showed his natural inclination to dig into a story, to see who was behind it," he says. "Once he got the connection to the

Army he really got going. It was a pleasure having a real reporter sitting across the room from you talking with enthusiasm about his work."

Following that story, Webb published a few more articles, one about a local measure aimed at funding local libraries in Sacramento, and a profile of a woman who helped people trying to sell houses redecorate their homes. His last story, a feature entitled "Red Light, Green Cash," exposed how local judges routinely upheld traffic violations cited by unreliable, privately owned cameras—exactly the type of muckraking journalism Webb had always craved.

Unbeknownst to Walsh, Webb was rapidly reaching the end of his dwindling psychological and financial resources. A major blow came when a Los Angeles television producer who was interested in hiring Webb to write a miniseries about arms trafficking backed out of the project. Webb had driven down to Los Angeles for a series of meetings and came back thinking the project was going to happen. When the deal fell apart, whatever hopes Webb had of resolving his financial difficulties and boosting his critically wounded ego evaporated and he sank even deeper into depression.

The last time Greg Wolf spoke to Webb was in May 2004. Over the course of the previous several weeks, they had exchanged a barrage of emails ranging from Wolf's refusal to get married to Webb's difficulties dating and the relative merits of various anti-depressant medications. Wolf knew Webb had developed a daily pot smoking habit, which he viewed as a form of self-medication, but became worried when Webb told him he was no longer taking his pills, because the side effects outweighed the benefits.

According to Wolf, Webb said his medication either made him feel numb or more depressed than he already was, and since he no longer had health insurance, he didn't want to pay for the pills out of his own pocket. "Man, that was some bad news," Wolf says. "He said he couldn't afford it, but that's bullshit. You can get Prozac for $30 a month. It was just a decision he made, and that's the last time I talked to him."

WEBB WASN'T EXAGGERATING his financial woes. In fact, he could no longer pay his bills. His new paycheck barely covered his monthly $2,000 mortgage, and shortly after he joined the *Sacramento News & Review*, Sue had garnished his wages for child support. She was already paying medical insurance for the three kids from her own paycheck and Webb hadn't sent her a dime for food, clothes, or other expenses since being laid off earlier that year. When Sue demanded $750 per month in child support, Webb emailed her back saying he couldn't afford it. "Obviously I cannot keep this job for very long," he said. "If I don't find something better, or sell the house, I'll be broke by Christmas."

His growing despair was fueled by the fact that his ex-girlfriend, whom he continued to pine after, refused to reciprocate his declarations of love. Although he continued to ride his motorcycle with his oldest son, Ian, he felt that his two younger children seemed to have too much going on in their lives to spend time with him. Webb was supposed to be able to share weekends with his kids, but they often had other plans. When they did stay at his house, Webb often stared blankly at his computer screen, playing video games.

"He didn't look good toward the end," Webb's brother, Kurt, says. "He had gained weight. He was getting in motorcycle accidents. He had taken up smoking more. He felt that everyone was against him. He didn't realize kids grow up and want to be on their own. He didn't feel needed anymore."

That fall, Webb's ex-girlfriend told his family that his depression had become so extreme that she worried he might harm himself. At the time, Sue and her kids thought that she was just being dramatic. But they were concerned enough to tell Webb's mother, who had recently moved from Orange County to a retirement community in Carmichael, so she could be closer to her son. "I immediately came down and tried to talk to him," Anita says. "But he closed himself off to me. He wouldn't talk. You couldn't start a conversation with him. He looked awful."

In early October Sue called Webb and left an angry message demanding that he start meeting his responsibilities—especially his financial ones—as a father. Webb didn't return Sue's call. Instead, on October 11, he emailed her. "I'm working on something that I think will solve all of your problems, and mine," he wrote. "Just give me a couple of weeks."

Three days later, Webb secretly purchased his cremation rights with a local funeral service. In mid-October he put his house on the market. "I was relieved he was going to sell it and start being able to pay child support," Sue says. She figured that selling his house was the plan he had mentioned that would solve both of their "problems."

Tom Walsh says Webb was slowly pulling away from his job, saying less in meetings and declining to elaborate on his ideas for future projects. When Webb didn't show up for work for several days in a row, Walsh called him for an explanation. "He was rather vague," Walsh says. "He said he had personal business to take care of. I called him again in a couple of days, and he said he had to sell his house and take off a couple of more days. On the third phone call, I said you have to come in and talk about this. He called me back and said he wanted to take some time off without pay. I was concerned about it and wanted to know how long he needed. He said he would get back to me." Walsh never spoke to Webb again.

At first Webb tried to avoid selling the house by refinancing his loan. He asked Kurt, a lawyer, for contacts, but when one loan failed to go through, he told his brother he was just going to sell the house. On Thanksgiving Day, Webb spent the holiday with Kurt's family. Usually, he'd play out at the pool with Kurt's kids. "We'd always relax and kick back," Kurt says. "He liked hanging out with my family."

But the dinner was a disaster: Kurt's wife got into a heated argument with her daughter and then stormed out of the house. He and his brother ended up watching a movie alone together, *Once Upon a Time in Mexico*. "That was the last movie we saw together," Kurt says. "He wasn't interested in the movie. He said he had to go." Later, Kurt figured that might have had something to do with the fact that one of the main characters, played by Johnny Depp, was a CIA agent.

Webb didn't have enough money to move into his own apartment right away. He begged his ex-girlfriend to let him stay with her. She said yes, but Webb called Sue in early

December, a week or so before his house was scheduled to clear escrow, and said his girlfriend wouldn't let him move in after all. Sue told him he had no choice but to live with his mother. According to Kurt, that was the last thing his brother would willingly do. "For some reason, he had this animosity towards her," he says. "He wouldn't have lasted long there."

In the week before he had to move in with his mother, Webb said goodbye to his ex-wife and kids. He spoke to Sue briefly about taking his daughter, Christine, to the doctor. When he brought her to the appointment, he playfully offered to read her *Green Eggs and Ham* in the waiting room. When he dropped her off at Sue's house, he handed her a bottle of perfume, but refused to come in the house.

Webb then asked his oldest son Ian to help him work on a motorcycle. Ian said he was busy, but Webb insisted. The last time Ian saw his father, they hung out in the garage for a few hours as Webb tried to fix his bike. "It was amazing to watch him work on bikes," Ian says. "I had no idea what he was doing. He was taking everything out and popping every-thing back in."

Ian was about to turn twenty-one, and Webb gave him an expensive watch as an early birthday present. "I was sur-prised because I knew he was pretty tight with money at the time, but I didn't want to second-guess him," he says. As Ian drove off on his motorcycle, Webb stood in his driveway, watching him leave. "It didn't really strike me as odd," he says. "He always liked to watch me drive away on the bike, but he kind of stayed there longer than usual. I guess he fig-ured it was the last time he was going to see me."

During the last few weeks of his life, Webb shut himself off from his family and his close friends. But he reached out to Annie Nocenti. For some reason, he felt she was the one person who could truly understand his pain. Besides being a former lover, Nocenti had worked on a suicide hotline. Webb told her that he was still in love with his ex-girlfriend and that she had refused to let him live with her. "He said he could not control his thoughts," Nocenti says. "He could not stop thinking about her. He was driving himself crazy."

To Nocenti, Webb seemed "situationally depressed." She felt that if he just got his ex-girlfriend out of his life, or planned a vacation somewhere, he'd be happy again. Webb told her he was contemplating a visit to New Zealand. Nocenti urged him to come visit her. When he refused, she offered to fly out to see him. Webb turned her down. "You'd stay for a week, we'd have fun, and then I'd put you on a plane and kill myself," he said.

Nocenti didn't think he was serious, but Webb called again and said he had decided to commit suicide. He'd already bought his cremation ticket, and told Nocenti he was holding a gun in his hands while they spoke. Webb made it clear he was speaking to her in strict confidence and that she could tell nobody about his plan. Nocenti tearfully begged Webb not to go through with his plan, and by the end of the conversation, she thought she he had cheered him up.

Just when she felt she had talked him out of suicide, Webb emailed Nocenti, saying that if she replied to his email and received an auto-reply, he was already dead. Over the next few days, Nocenti kept emailing Webb, but he didn't respond. To her horror, she got an auto-reply on Thursday,

December 9. When Webb didn't answer his phone all that day, Nocenti began obsessively typing his name on the Google search page, looking for evidence that he had finally followed through on his threats.

Webb hadn't answered Nocenti's calls that day because he was busy putting his belongings in a storage shed at his mother's house. Halfway through the task, his bike broke down, and as would later become clear, the man who gave Webb a lift home had stolen it by the time he got back with a tow truck. With his description of the man, the police were able to arrest the thief and retrieve Webb's bike three days later. Webb spent several hours at his mother's house that evening, unable to say anything except that he didn't see much a future for himself.

"He had no idea how he was going to make a living," Anita says. "He said he couldn't write anymore. I told him he was already working for a newspaper, but he had an ego and wanted to write for very big newspapers. He was so despondent. He could see nothing at the end. I couldn't talk him out of the depths of his despair."

Webb planned his suicide with the same attention to detail and relentless determination that he brought to "Dark Alliance." He had sold his house, packed his belongings, said goodbye to his family, paid in advance for his own cremation, and left his driver's license next to his bed so that nobody in his family would have to identify his body. Although it's impossible to know if it was deliberate, the morning after he said goodbye to his mother, December 10, 2004—when the movers arrived at his house and found the note on his front door telling them to call the ambulance—marked seven years to the day since Gary Webb had resigned from the *San Jose Mercury News*.

EPILOGUE

GARY WEBB'S SUICIDE didn't go
unnoticed in the industry to which he had dedicated the better part of his life. But unlike "Dark Alliance," it wasn't
front-page news. "Gary Webb, a prize winning investigative
journalist whose star-crossed career was capped with a
controversial newspaper series linking the CIA to the crack-
cocaine epidemic in Los Angeles, died Friday of self-
inflicted gunshot wounds," the *Sacramento Bee* reported in
a December 12 obituary. "Three of the nation's leading
newspapers, the *New York Times*, the *Los Angeles Times*
and the *Washington Post*, followed up with reports questioning Mr. Webb's conclusions, and eventually his own
newspaper turned on him."

Three days later, *The Bee* published a follow-up story

intending to quell rumors then spreading throughout conspiracy Web sites on the Internet that the CIA had assassinated Webb. "Such a case normally would have sparked little notice," The *Bee* reported. "But Webb's allegations spawned a following, including conspiracy theorists who have worked the Internet feverishly for days with notions that because Webb died from two gunshots he was killed by government agents or the contras in retribution for the stories written nearly a decade ago."

Perhaps the most absurd account of Webb's supposed murder came from Prisonplanet.com, an Austin, Texas based Internet radio show run by Alex Jones. Under a headline "The Murder of Gary Webb," Jones darkly referred to "credible sources who were close to Gary Webb" and who said he was working on a new exposé involving the CIA. According to Jones' sources, Webb "was receiving death threats, being regularly followed," and "he was concerned about strange individuals who were seen on multiple occasions breaking into and leaving his house."

Jones claimed that Webb had recently complained about intruders "who were obviously not burglars but government people." When Webb confronted them, these "professionals" escaped by "jumping from his balcony" and "scaling down the pipes outside his home." The only problem with that scenario is that Webb lived in a one-story ranch house with no balcony or pipes on the wall.

Sue didn't find out that her ex-husband had shot himself twice until she got a call from the *Bee* reporter who wrote that story. She later discovered that Webb almost didn't succeed in killing himself. When the first bullet pierced his cheek, it missed his brain, tearing only soft tissue. Webb pulled the trigger again. The second bullet barely nicked an artery, and Webb, who likely fell unconscious moments later, ultimately bled to death.

It was hardly the mark of a professional hit. Sue told the reporter she was certain her ex-husband had committed suicide. "The way he was acting, it would be hard for me to believe it was anything but suicide," she said, explaining that he had been "distraught for some time over his inability to get a job at another major newspaper."

Sue also received a call from a San Francisco-based private investigator who said he had been hired to investigate her ex-husband's death. He wanted a hair sample, explaining that there might be chemical traces in his hair follicles that would show whether he had been murdered. Sue agreed to meet the man at the mortuary, where she reluctantly provided him with a sample. Later, the investigator called her and asked if Sue would agree to an autopsy if he could raise the money. She said she'd think it over.

The investigator called back on the day of the memorial service and said he had raised $6,000. He asked for her permission to collect Webb's body. "I told him it was too late, that he had already been cremated," Sue says. "But there was no reason to have an autopsy. I don't know what happened to that hair sample. I never got a call."

That wasn't the last of it, however. Nearly a year after Webb's death, Anita Langley, host of Black Op Radio, an Internet radio broadcast devoted to conspiracy topics, emailed Sue. Langley claimed that Webb was in contact with witnesses to unspecified secret government operations shortly before he died. Government agents recently had murdered some of those witnesses and their entire families, she said.

"Gary would have known that these people kill children," Langley wrote. "If he wrote the suicide notes, I think it is possible he would have done so as a result of being given the option to spare his children a terrible fate . . . Gary learned about the worst types of crimes imaginable, and I do suppose it is possible that his death was a suicide, but in light of what I have told you, I hope you will consider the possibility that there may have been a professional hit here."

Langley asked Sue to search Gary's records for any notes that would confirm these contacts. In an email, Langley told me she had no proof to support her suspicions, but is certain Webb was digging into a story that could have caused powerful government forces to threaten him. Sue and Webb's son Ian, however, dug through Webb's documents, and found nothing to indicate he was working on anything other than stories for the *Sacramento News & Review*.

There wasn't any assassin's bullet, nor was there any need for one. It was Gary Webb's controversial, career-ending story—and the combined resources and dedication of America's three largest and most powerful newspapers—that killed his career as a reporter and set the stage for his personal self-destruction. Without exception, those who knew Webb well believe he killed himself. And while the reasons they offer for that belief differ in terms of the precipitant motivation for Webb's decision to commit suicide, they converge on one point: Webb's depression may have existed for decades on one level or another, but it only became life-threatening after his banishment from journalism thanks to the controversy over "Dark Alliance."

Journalists who helped expose the connection between the CIA, the Nicaraguan contras, and drug smuggling say that while "Dark Alliance" wasn't a perfect piece of journalism, Gary Webb deserves to be celebrated for forcing the CIA to admit that it had protected contra drug smugglers from prosecution and then lied about it for years. They mourn the fact that Webb paid such a heavy price for one story, however controversial.

"What happened to Gary is an American tragedy, but one that still hasn't been addressed," says Bob Parry, the AP reporter who originally broke the contra-cocaine story. "I'm stunned at how mean the mainstream press has chosen to be. [They are] so lacking of any self criticism about this. The press has displayed much more self criticism on such smaller issues, but there's been no self criticism on this one."

"A good editor would have made Gary modify his conclusions," says the *Nation*'s David Corn. "This would have saved 'Dark Alliance,' and perhaps saved Gary. He would have gone on with his life. It was an explosive story because it over-reached. It's fair to assume had it not overreached it would have been better for him. But because it overreached those Inspector General reports came out. One thing Gary should be remembered for is that his pursuit of this issue did cause huge chunks of the truth to come out of the CIA."

"I don't know why he killed himself or what would have prevented that," says Marc Cooper of *LA Weekly*. "What I can say is that the media killed his career. That's obvious and it's really a nauseating and very discouraging story, because as a journalist, the only thing you have is your credibility. When that is shredded, there's no way to rebuild it."

Cooper agrees with Corn that "Dark Alliance" contained serious flaws, but reserves special scorn for the journalists who criticized his story. "If Gary Webb made mistakes I have no problem with exposing them," he says. "But given the sweep of American journalism over the past fifty years, this is an outstanding case where three of the major newspapers in the country decided to take out somebody, a competitor whose mistakes seem by any measure to be very minor."

French journalist Paul Moreira, who interviewed Webb in 1997, filmed a forty-five-minute documentary about Webb for the investigative program *90 Minutes* on France's Canal Plus—the only televised coverage of his suicide anywhere in the world. Moreira also interviewed *Washington Post* reporter Walter Pincus about the media's lack of coverage on the CIA's inspector general report admitting the agency worked with drug dealers throughout the 1980s.

"It was much, much more grave than Watergate," Moreira says. "The report comes out precisely in the middle of all the noise around Monica and Bill, and no one pays attention! That's when I discovered that media-noise is the new censorship." Moreira says his bosses weren't overjoyed about broadcasting his documentary. "They thought it was too distant for the French, and they were right; the ratings were not that good," he says. (Shortly after this interview, Canal Plus cancelled the show). "But somehow I knew I was doing the right thing. I felt like justice should be given to his work, his name. Not enough people in this job are ready to take some risks. He did."

The *Post's* Pincus says Webb was ultimately a victim of his own celebrity, not other journalists. "One thing I have been fascinated with is what notoriety does to people who have never felt it," he says. "The fifteen minutes of fame business is really dangerous. There are people who fawn all over you, who make you think you are much more important than you really are. It happens in this city all the time."

Pincus believes that the most important legacy of "Dark Alliance" was that the story—along with other scandals that plagued the agency in the 1990s, including its ties to a Guatemalan Army officer who murdered a left-wing rebel married to U.S. citizen Jennifer Harbury—encouraged the CIA to be less aggressive in its efforts against Islamic terrorism, which helped enable Osama bin Laden's 9/11 terrorist attacks.

"That's horseshit," says Jack Blum, who headed Senator Kerry's subcommittee on narcotics and terrorism during the 1980s. "The CIA and FBI didn't stop 9/11 because nobody listened to their agents in the field. And the disease that led the mainstream media to dump all over Gary Webb is the same disease that led the media to be so uncritical about the Iraq war. This guy was abused for doing his job. To the extent he was wrong, the fault lies with his editors who probably didn't work with him sufficiently or do certain checking on some of the stuff he was told."

Greg Wolf believes his lifelong friend died because he stopped taking his anti-depressants. "This has got nothing to do with politics or his career, but brain chemistry," he says. "He was clinically depressed. He was having a continuous midlife crisis and that's what killed him." But Wolf suspects that "Dark Alliance" was the central cause of Webb's depression. "That story was his first big hit of crystal meth," he says. "And then he was no longer just some respected reporter, he was a celebrity. And they took that away from him and it was too much for him. He wrote the biggest story of his life and then he was a pariah."

"He was a courageous guy, but too stubborn for his own good—and paid the price," says Tom Loftus, one of Webb's friends from the *Kentucky Post*. "I've never seen an investigative project come under fire like 'Dark Alliance.' It hasn't happened before or since. I wonder how many Pulitzer prizes would be revoked in the *Washington Post* or *New York Times* if those papers used their best reporters to examine each other. Now all his editors have better jobs and the reporter is dead."

Tom Scheffey, who co-authored the Coal Connection articles with Webb at the *Kentucky Post*, believes Webb's editors at the *Mercury News* betrayed him. "I think that being an investigative reporter is like being a trained Doberman," he says. "All their training goes into being good at sniffing things out, running at the ground, and going after the story. For inexplicable reasons, after all these instincts and talents are built in, the chain is jerked. This is what drives Dobermans and investigative reporters nuts—getting really good at something and then being told you can't do it. Gary was betrayed by his handlers."

Tom Andrzejewski—the Polish-American reporter who always thought every phone call was "The Big One"—asserts that anybody who would claim to know the truth behind the dark events Webb chronicled in his big story is misguided.

"Somewhere in there was the truth," he says. "Gary probably got close to it. The problem was he couldn't prove it." Andrzejewski believes the attacks Webb endured were "the beginning of the end" for his friend. "It was such an egregious, mean-spirited response," he says. "The way the respected papers took him on and treated him so shabbily was unprecedented."

Anita Webb, the last person to speak with her son before he shot himself, says she will never forgive the journalists who spent so much time and energy attacking Gary Webb. "They destroyed my son's career," she says. "Gary was an honest reporter, and they killed him. I'll never forgive the people who destroyed my son."

The mainstream media's attacks continued even after Webb's suicide. On December 12, the *Los Angeles Times*, which had done more than any other newspaper to destroy Webb's career eight years earlier, published a brief obituary saying his work on the CIA and drugs had been "discredited." The source for this alleged discrediting was, of course, the *Times* itself. The obituary writers, Nita Lelyveld and Steve Hymon, looked no further than the paper's own response to "Dark Alliance."

Bob Parry recalls learning of Webb's suicide from the *LA Times*, which called him for a comment. Parry told the reporter that the American people owed a "huge debt" to Gary Webb for exposing an important, dark chapter in their country's history. "I said you'll have trouble writing about it accurately, because if you look at your paper's clips you'll have trouble finding a single accurate story about what he exposed," Parry says.

The *San Jose Mercury News* finally acknowledged its role in Webb's tragic fate in a December 16 editorial. "After any suicide, survivors feel guilty," wrote Scott Herhold, the editor who worked with Webb in his early years at the *Mercury News*. "Was there any way it could have been avoided?" Webb, he said, was an "immensely talented reporter, a good writer and a sometimes-difficult human being. In many ways he represented the best of our craft—its compassion, its obligation to speak truth to power."

Herhold also wrote that Webb's "lack of doubt" in his beliefs "demanded a firm editor to challenge him. "Gary didn't get that on any level . . . 'Dark Alliance' was as much an institutional failure as it was a personal one. Yet Webb bore the chief consequences." Herhold refused to comment on a claim by a former *Mercury News* reporter that the paper killed an additional line in his obituary stating that while Webb lost his job over "Dark Alliance," all of the editors who worked on that story were later promoted.

"The zeal that helped make Gary a relentless reporter was coupled with an inability to question himself, to entertain the notion that he might have erred," says former *Mercury News* editor Jonathan Krim. He wonders if Gary's reaction to criticism allowed other people involved in his story—like his editors—to escape harsher scrutiny. "There was plenty of responsibility to go around," he concludes. "We failed as a newspaper."

Dawn Garcia emerged from the "Dark Alliance" controversy with her career intact. In 2000, she left the *Mercury News* and rejoined her alma mater as deputy director for Stanford University's John S. Knight Fellowships for

Professional Journalists. Garcia never kept in touch with Webb after he left the paper, but according to Webb's former colleague, Pamela Kramer, Webb told her shortly before his death that he didn't blame Garcia for what happened to his career.

Unlike the other editors who handled the project, Garcia recognizes her own failures. "Had I to do all over again, I would have pushed to hold the story until everything was truly ready," she says. "I would have recast parts of the series to focus on the very strong reporting Gary had done, and be much more careful about how we worded the conclusions of that reporting." Garcia believes "the core of the series was correct but that the conclusions Gary drew were too sweeping. We could have had almost as strong or stronger a story by being more explanatory in what we thought and why we thought so."

But Garcia also feels the "Dark Alliance" controversy helped reveal an important part of U.S. history that had been largely ignored by the American media. "Two years after the series ran, a CIA Inspector General's report acknowledged that the CIA had indeed worked with suspected drug runners while supporting the contras," she says. "The IG report would not have happened if 'Dark Alliance' had not been published. I also think we began a long overdue investigation into a dark chapter of U.S. policy. We raised important questions about what the government knew about drug smuggling that hadn't been covered well by the media."

Managing Editor David Yarnold, who stopped reading Webb's story halfway through the editing process, rose to become executive editor, then editor of the paper's opinion section. He left the *Mercury News* in 2005 and is now director of an environmental organization in New York City. Paul Van Slambrouck, who replaced Yarnold on the story, was promoted to a corporate position with Knight Ridder before becoming editor of the *Christian Science Monitor*. In 2003, the *Monitor* published a story based on forged documents accusing George Galloway, a left-wing member of the British parliament, of accepting millions of dollars from Saddam Hussein during the 1990s. After issuing a formal apology to Galloway, Van Slambrouck stepped down as editor and became a San Francisco-based correspondent for the paper.

In 1997, Jerry Ceppos received the Society of Professional Journalists' Ethics in Journalism award for publishing his mea culpa about "Dark Alliance." Two years later, he left the *Mercury News* to become vice president for news at Knight Ridder. Ceppos celebrated his final day in journalism on August 31, 2005, taking an early retirement to enjoy his vineyard in Saratoga.

Had he lived, Gary Webb would have turned fifty years old that day. Two weeks later, his family—Sue, Anita, Kurt, Ian, Eric, and Christine—marked Webb's birthday by driving to Santa Cruz Bay. With the Rolling Stones song, "You Can't Always Get What You Want," blaring from a boom box, they obeyed his final wish—and let him bodysurf for eternity.

They tossed his ashes into the crashing waves of the Pacific.

AUTHOR'S ACKNOWLEDGMENTS

KILL THE MESSENGER shares its title with a December 2004 obituary I wrote about Gary Webb for *OC Weekly*. As I wrote at the time, I knew Gary through his "Dark Alliance" story. Shortly after I published a follow-up article to his 1996 *San Jose Mercury News* series, Webb called me to thank me for advancing his reporting. Over the next several years, I wrote numerous investigative stories concerning members of the drug ring he exposed; Webb used much of the material I uncovered in his 1998 book, *Dark Alliance*. (Unless otherwise indicated, all quotes attributed to Webb come from his book).

I met Webb just once, during his 1998 book tour, but kept in touch with him until shortly before his death. I should also point out that in 1993, I worked for three months as an intern for David Corn, Washington editor of the *Nation* magazine, who as this book shows, both criticized and defended Webb's reporting.

Kill the Messenger would not have been possible without the cooperation of many people, but especially Webb's family: Susan, Ian, Kurt, and Anita. I would also like to thank everyone else who spoke to me for this project—Webb's friends, colleagues, supporters, and particularly his detractors, who did so despite their knowledge that my book entailed a serious critique of their coverage of the "Dark Alliance" scandal: Tom Andrzejewski, Jeremy Bigwood, Jack Blum, Walt Bogdanich, Pete Carey, Gary Clark, Alexander Cockburn, Marc Cooper, David Corn, Mike Crosby, Rex Davenport, Tom Dresslar, Dawn Garcia, Tim Golden, Lee Gomes, Scott Herhold, Martha Honey, Jesse Katz, Chris Knap, Peter Kornbluh, Pamela Kramer, Jonathan Krim, Howard Kurtz, Tom Loftus, Steve Luttner, Joe Madison, Doyle McManus, Paul Moreira, Annie Nocenti, Bob Parry, Walter Pincus, Bert Robinson, Mike Ruppert, Adam Saytanides, Tom Scheffey, Mary Anne Sharkey, Dan Simon, Tom Suddes, Vance Trimble, Sanho Tree, Tom Walsh, Leo Wolinsky, and Greg Wolf.

I'd also like to thank my former editor at *OC Weekly*, Will Swaim, who tutored me as a writer and investigative reporter for the past decade, and who encouraged me in this project. Jesse Fenichel and my wife Claudia Schou provided invaluable support by reading early drafts of this manuscript, and Charles Bowden generously allowed me use of his unpublished notes from his 1998 interview with Webb for *Esquire* Magazine.

I owe a special debt of gratitude to Mike Davis at the University of California, Irvine, who inspired me to write this book and helped me find a publisher, and to my editors, Ruth Baldwin and Carl Bromley, for believing in this story and trusting in my ability to do it justice. Special thanks to Peter Landesman, Naomi Despres, Scott Stuber, Jeremy Renner and his producing partner at The Combine, Don Handfield, Michael Cuesta, and everyone at Focus Features who helped make the filming of this book possible. More than anything else, *Kill the Messenger* owes its origin to a talented journalist who tragically, will never read it. "From one newsman to another—keep the faith," Webb once told me. I only wish that somehow he had been able to do the same.

 # The Nation Institute

Founded in 2000, **Nation Books** has become a leading voice in American independent publishing. The inspiration for the imprint came from the *Nation* magazine, the oldest independent and continuously published weekly magazine of politics and culture in the United States.

The imprint's mission is to produce authoritative books that break new ground and shed light on current social and political issues. We publish established authors who are leaders in their area of expertise, and endeavor to cultivate a new generation of emerging and talented writers. With each of our books we aim to positively affect cultural and political discourse.

Nation Books is a project of The Nation Institute, a nonprofit media center dedicated to strengthening the independent press and advancing social justice and civil rights. The Nation Institute is home to a dynamic range of programs: the award-winning Investigative Fund, which supports groundbreaking investigative journalism; the widely read and syndicated website TomDispatch; the Victor S. Navasky Internship Program in conjunction with the *Nation* magazine; and Journalism Fellowships that support up to 25 high-profile reporters every year.

For more information on Nation Books, The Nation Institute, and the *Nation* magazine, please visit:

www.nationbooks.org

www.nationinstitute.org

www.thenation.com

www.facebook.com/nationbooks.ny

Twitter: @nationbooks